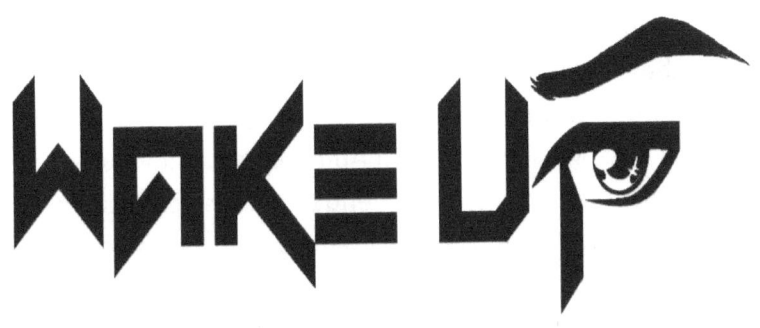

Financial independence and business ownership is to the African American people today as freedom was to our African ancestors when they were in chains. A distant dream.

AWAKEN THE ENTREPRENEUR
SPIRIT

DEON ABDULLAH

Dedication

I dedicate this book to my beautiful wife Nahstassia Abdullah, my three children, Nia, Cameron and Amyr Abdullah. They have been a strong foundation and continuous line of support for me on this project. My brothers Rashad Abdullah, Adam Abdullah and Jeran Wade gave me a lot of creative insight on my project. My parents Tracy Batson-Allen and Alim Abdullah have always supported me in my writing endeavors and critique the ideas I write about. Natisha Haynie receives a huge thanks from me for her advice and wisdom and it was because of her I was able to start on this book.

I was inspired to write this book from my past. As a child, I always tried to decipher God's strategic layout which I have accepted is above the human beings cardinal mind. I now come to understood his desire and that is for mankind to constantly evolve into its true potential, to wake up all my brothers and sisters to continue the fight for true freedom. Our ancestors had fought through slavery and civil rights, now it is my generations turn to continue the battle to fight for a real slice of the American dream.

The pursuit of happiness is that very definition. The pursuit! The fact is with only wanting to be successful but deny risk is like trying to catch a star at night with your hand, it seems like it's right in your hands yet it is so far away. We each have an obligation to be a pillar in our community and hold our weight in this free enterprise market or risk being entirely consumed in other businesses. When you own your business, you own a great portion of your life where you dictate your agenda. Get off the bench and into the game, leave the corporate army and from your own empire, take your dreams in put it in a business plan. We must be the change we want and try something new besides the old traditional way of thinking. To all my brothers and sisters black or any other race, I urge you to take hold of your life and steer it into your fantasies!

Warning!!

Please read the following setting and character explanation. This is a point of view book with more than one perspective. This book shifts between characters during the plot. This quick rundown will give you more insight to the story. I hope you enjoy the reading as much as I enjoyed writing it.

Deon Abdullah

Saints Grove

Saints Grove is a fictional place based in Tacoma Washington. Saints Grove is a symbolic place that represents many Black neighborhoods across America. The people portrayed in this city represent certain groups within the black community and the mentalities they have towards life. Even though these are fictional people and the events are created, they are derived from actual events and people.

Darrius

The main character and ultimate narrator of the book. Darrius is a veteran that has found his way back home to Saints Grove. He is married to Chelsea; his brother is Jeff and is a cousin to Roman. He constantly finds himself dreaming of better life alternatives to his current situation. Darrius questions his community's motives and understanding of the African American race as a whole. He is a writer at heart but is wrapped up in his day to day life and the people he surrounds himself with until Omar tasks him with a series of assignments.

Roman

Roman is a character wrapped up with the risky fast pace life of the underground drug world. He is 2 Tone/ Andre's right hand man and has a distorted view about life until his eyes are opened by the teachings of Omar.

2 Tone/ Andre

Andre also known by his street name 2 Tone is a character stuck in his ways bent on social alienation from society. He lives by his own rules and uses life misfortunes as a platform to stand on when he justifies going against societal norms, rules and regulations. He is the ultimate leader of his underground enterprise, Romans partner and is a childhood friend of Darrius.

Omar

Omar is Andre's father that got lost in the criminal justice system when he was locked up for all of Andre's life. He starts the book off as a recently freed man and is focused on reviving the African American community from the trenches to prosperity. He befriends Aamira in prison during a prison program.

Stone

Stone is a White detective that prides himself on being a law enforcer. He is partnered with Cordell and they are tasked with finding the trigger man of the heinous crime that slayed a little girl during a drive by shooting. He has a tainted view of the people of Saints Grove due to the high crime rate and lack of progression. He finds himself like Darrius questioning the mindset of the African American community.

Aamira

Aamira is a Muslim woman who is the mother of Ali and grandmother of the deceased little girl. She is an immigrant from Ethiopia and is feed up with the status of the black population. She befriends Omar and together set a plan in motion to rekindle the fire for the people of Saints Grove

LaShandria

LaShandria is the girlfriend of Roman. She is a woman that had such promise in her past but she feels her love for Roman and affiliation with Saints Grove has devoured her potential and thus has her living a mediocre life. She and Roman have one daughter together.

Cordell

Cordell is the Partner of Stone and has a shady side as he does business for the badge and behind the badge with the underground kingpins.

Bone/ Michael

Michael also known by his street name Bone is one of Andre and Roman's accomplice in the criminal world. He makes the majority of his living as a stereo man hooking up sound systems in client's vehicles at Dave's auto shop.

Ali

Ali is the father of the deceased little girl and is 2 Tone's rival. He is hell bent on pursuing revenge for his loss. He is the son of Aamira.

Chelsea

Chelsea is the wife of Darrius and is pregnant throughout most of the book. You will hear her many times referred to as the roommate by Darrius because of their constant absents and lack of connection between the two.

Jeff

Jeff is the brother of Darrius and is living life with no ambition.

Roger

Roger is a close friend of Jeff and one of Andre's best street dealers. He was put on to the street life by Roman.

Tasha

Tasha is a military comrade of Darrius during his enlistment. She is married to Mike another one of Darrius's friends and she is going through a painful breakup with her husband. She confides in Darrius.

Mr. Taylor

Mr. Taylor is one of the oldest black business owners that is devoted to serving his community. He is a respected member of the community even though the neighborhood has turned their support away from his restaurant for cheaper products in fast-food.

Lisa

Lisa is Darrius's coworker with a submissive type demeanor. She constantly takes the blunt of people's aggression and is compared to a punching bag at work.

Alisha

Alisha is Darrius's classmate from a more privilege upper class neighborhood north of Saints Grove. Her and Darrius are the only two black people in their class and they form a bond based on that similarity.

Fred

Fred is another comrade of Darrius from his military days. He is a street gang member from California who befriends Darrius during their enlistment. Although Fred's military obligation is terminated premature of his original contract due to his behavior he and Darrius still remain in contact.

Chapter 1

Omar

The air is cool carrying the flavors of pine cones, the soft dirt and grass under my feet are dripping in morning dew. The whistling of the wind, dancing of the trees and animals going about their day give harmony to the wilderness. The dense vegetation blocks out the sound of the freeways, traffic congestion and emergency sirens even though it's a half a mile away.

"This place has always been a sanctuary where I can clear my head and look at things from a different perspective. Growing up the only thing I could hear was the sound of my stomach rumbling, you see people don't know how powerful hunger is. It can control your whole mind set, and put actions in motion you would never think you was capable of. Anything is justifiable when you hungry and morals are for the obese. Hunger enslaves you and the risk you take to fulfill your self is given to you by justification."

She stands still taking in the scenery and does a slight head nod to let me know she is listening. She always seemed to do that even when there wasn't any scenery to look at when I met her in prison. She ran a program that explained Islam to prisoners. I had to be locked in a cage before I could find freedom.

"It's funny the one thing that people like me have that served time is true appreciation for the taste of freedom. 23 years I stayed isolated from the outside world and yet I feel I have more of an understanding than many people walking that have never been handcuffed."

She smiles, the type of smile that reassures you. The person that she stood next to was quite different when she first met me.

When we first crossed paths. She received the blunt of my anger, as I was cursing God for why he had set me up for failure. Nothing of luxury or even necessity was at my disposal. Clothes where scrapes from others wardrobes to make room for new designer clothing, shoes where passed on to me after they had been worn for a time and then converted into lawn cutting shoes before I would acquire them. It seemed the only thing that was given to me was the view of how life should be. TV showed full families with massive dinner spreads, nice cars, warm beds and attentive parents. It seemed I could only bear witness to the treasures. It took only one time for me to get addicted to the shadow life.

I was hungrier than ever one day when I had walked into the convenient store, God that candy looked so good. The bottled orange juice looked like it could cure days of thirst. I was so nervous that I walk back out the store and stood on the side for a long while. The close proximity to the food only made my desires grow to the point I used every ounce of courage to run in there a snatch as much as I could grab. I ran clear across town before I nearly collapse from exhaustion. Till this day, I had never had a better candy bar and bottle of orange juice. Stealing did for me what a day in school, chores and responsibility couldn't do, feed me.

It wasn't enough to be satisfied however, I had to eat as though I was preparing for hibernation, and excess became my motivation turning my hunger into greed. The newest pair of shoes had to purchase and the latest trends had to be on me. The grind brought not only full dinner tables, but power that commanded others to follow and do my bidding and women that could satisfy even the fullest man. A woman beyond the word beautiful consumed my heart and I gave her my seed on new year's day. That was back in the 80's before my actions finally caught up with me on April 23, 1989. They say a man that is starving is one of the worst forms of torture but I say a starving man turned full and is lead back to starvation is the worst of all. They surrounded me with bars with only myself and my anger. The letters only came for a short time from the woman that stole my heart only informing me that she named him Andre.

She freed me those days, I would sit in her class and a little after her lessons were done. The power of the mind overcame my hunger and filled me up in ways I could never imagine. My life is in her debt.

"He is here you know" she says finally breaking her silence.

The air feels even colder knowing that me connecting with my boy as a grown man is slim to none.

"He is the spitting image of you and your past." She continues.

"How am I supposed to connect with him sister?"

"The streets have grown worst believe it or not Omar, children are groomed to be criminals, innocence of a child is short lived before the wrath of reality take hold of them giving them cheat sheets to success but sooner or later a cheater always gets caught. The lessons are never learned they just find ways to cheat the system. Your son is harden by his environment so the way to change him is to change the atmosphere he resides." She stated

"How am I to do that?"

"By getting them to wake up. I fall short with my teachings to the younger generation but over the years I see you have the voice that people listen to. Your son, my son and almost every other person in Saints grove need these lessons. Wake them up.

Chapter 2

Roman

"Ok yall niggas ready?" Tone says over the loud music.

"Man I stay ready! You need to ask ya mans over here sweatin and shit!" Bone responds

"Man shut the fuck up Bone and just drive, lets hurry up and get this shit over wit."

The ford explore had a smooth ride gliding over the rough pavement. Y.G. was pouring through the speakers mesmerizing us in the lyrics. The glock was on fire with one in the chamber, even though my palms are sweating with the heat blasting, my hands fill as though I was holding on to ice.

"here nigga take a shot of this, it will calm your ass down."

He shoves the bottle of Henney in my hands, The throat burn warms my body as the spirits drain into me to the point I gag, back washing into the bottle.

"Damn nigga give me my shit back wastin the shit." Tone snaps.

I wipe my mouth only to make my face wetter with sweat that smelled like metal from me griping the gun so hard. The car slows to a creep as my heart begins to race; my window is facing the target house. Bone rolls down the window and his barrel points outside. I stand up on the back seat and raise up out the sun roof. We both spray the house punching holes in the walls and shattering the windows! I can hear the sounds of screaming in between the shots. The loud screeching of the tires accelerates us into the next block speeding off into the night.

Aamira/ Muslim Lady

The phone lights up in the darkness, the sound piercing the silent of the night. It was awkwardly quiet from the beginning, no bass rumbling, police and ambulance sirens nor loud house parties. It's no wonder why I couldn't sleep in the first place; the pure silence allows my mind to think so loudly that sleep is impossible. The hour is late but the night is young, the people suffering trying to walk favorably in society go to sleep while the stereotypes face off with society. The phone still rings but it's far too late to be calling someone like me. I've picked up these phone calls in the past and tragedy is always the caller. Despair has always been my families close neighbor, most of my nephews have been enslaved by the system, and many of my nieces either entrapped by the system or depended on it. My daughter indulges in the devil's sugar, consuming it every chance she gets, she obsessed with it. I've heard of her many times exchanging her body for another high while my son is a whole different story. You see he is one of the devil's soldiers that do his bidding. The same thing his sister gives her life for is the same thing he sells for 40 bucks a gram. My children know nothing of the turbulent past from our time in Ethiopia, they were too young to remember the journey to America, and their lives as they know it started in Saints Grove. A place where they were ridiculed by the black kids for being too black, the longer we resided in Saints Grove the more the African population grew forming two types of black communities in the same neighborhood. They couldn't see that there histories united and that they were the demise to their own future. In my mind the black community as a whole has given the white man way to much credit for our current predicament.

The phone still rings as I went through every possible shred of bad news I could think of to prepare myself for the voice on the other end. I reach over the Quran on my night stand to grab my phone. I see Ali on my caller ID.

"Hello"

"Mom I need you to come over here and get my kids I have to take Jessica to the hospital. "

Ali had always been ashamed of his Islamic roots, him and his sisters where teased all the time for the way they dressed. It's no wonder why he named his first daughter Jessica a name far away from traditional Muslim type names. No matter I loved her and my other grandkids the same.

"What happened Ali why is she going to the hospital?"

I can hear the crackling in his voice, the reluctant tone he had letting me know he dread his words to come.

"She, she, she got shot mom! She got shot!"

I don't need any further explanation; I know what happened and how it happened. The life Ali choose to reside in brought fast money, women to envy, life's material treasures and pain. The bullets were sent from someone wanting to make a point. I never understood why these young men found respect in taking lives, something that's easy to do. They disrespect the people who support and break there back trying to maintain life while idolizing the very people who degrade our reputation into stereotypes that bring us all down. Ali understands this however, his lessons are always understood with examples and my granddaughter had to be that lesson. If I know my son then I know what Ali's next actions will be; I know that compassion won't come out of his daughter's tragedy but rage against his own people. Only more pain will satisfy his own.

"Okay son I'm on my way."

Right after I hang up I dial Omar's number. He needs to start, his timing is far late but he needs to begin now!

Darrius

To say this was how this story started would be inaccurate, for violence, division and self-destruction has harassed my people way before my birth. But for me this story started that horrible night Jessica was slayed, a little girl that paid the debt of her father by being in the wrong place at the wrong time. Some say that the best way to tell a story is to tell the beginning and the end and then go through the how's, whys and what's. As I look over the events that led to our communities awakening I see the conclusion in the form of a face off.

Roman

My hands are pulsating, sore to the bone with skinless knuckles when I connected to his jaw line snagging his teeth as my hand followed through. My mind is full of rage and my heart with pain, I want to hit more than just him but we are the only two present! I lunge at him again hoping to draw more blood but instead get caught with a blow to the gut making me remember what I had to eat an hour ago. The agony brings me to my knees spitting up stomach acid. I catch a size ten and a half Timberland to the face at the same time I catch my breath lifting my head up to the sky with gravity bringing me down on my back. Warm fluid runs out the side of my mouth as I spit vomit and blood out.

"I told you Nigga not to fuck with me" He screamed

I gather my vision back and struggle to my feet. The cold air numbs my face while the swelling and blood thaws in the same area making my face painfully cold.

"I told you I'm out and I don't care if I go down with you, I can't let niggas like you make us all niggas! Omar was wrong, everybody can't be saved!" I screamed

When I thought off my childhood he held the majority of my memories. A person I would had caught a bullet for or did anything to avenge if wrong was thrown his way was now a person I wanted to take out of this world.

"You a fake ass nigga just like that preachin nigga Omar! And I tell you what, ya female that you think is on some loyal shit is the fakest of them all. Let just say I know her in and out Cuz!" He confesses.

I know what he means, I know what she had done, and I know when it all went wrong. The circle of blame had me in the center of my own demise and betrayal. I didn't care, her sin came from weakness, emotion and insecurity his sin however was insidious and backstabbing. The adrenalin ran through my blood stream, my fist clenched so hard that my fingers indented my palm, as I ran at him with everything that wasn't already shed from the previous blows.

2 Tone

I relive my waist band of the weight I always carried on me. The steel is warm from my body heat in the cold night. The man that's coming at me is one of hate and I should know because I created this; If he is the hero of this story I am surely the antagonist. What the hell is good anyway? I mean hell to the upper class white male America is Heaven sent, a place of heroes; But if you ask my grandfather and his father before him America is slavery, if you ask a native American, America are made of thieves, you ask the British back in the day America are an assemble of traitors, and if you ask China, America is forever in debt. So what is right in this world full of wrong because if you ask me if everyone around you is wrong and you the only one right then you're the crazy one. I can't believe he is still running at me with this barrel staring at him

I should have known this would have ended like this. I could had convinced this nigga to do anything so I should had foretold that someone else one day would convince his mind of something else. He wanted me to change with him but my mind isn't open like his. My mind is locked on this money and just because the government can't tax my shit they want to call it illegal and me a felon. Omar getting the whole block riled up talking about capital, and assets and shit. All his jaw jackin finally engulfed the man charging at me and to him I'm now an obstacle to progress. As for me filling up his lady I did him a favor, showing him not to waste his time with these females. All it took was a few words to capture her, I exploited her weakness and he is mad at me. I'm just the one who found out for him, you don't get mad at the doc for finding the disease, you just rid yourself of it. My fingers grip the trigger tighter the closer he gets, I don't want to but I have to survive.

Lashandria

My head slams on the dash board as the sudden stop pinball my head in the car. The sound was so loud it acted as a stop sign halting us to a screeching stop. The sound that rings throughout the neighborhood is familiar during the fourth of July or new year's in most communities but here it would be a surprise if it were ever a firework.

I didn't mean the things I use to say about him. For so long I saw him as the person who blocked my opportunity when in reality he was the door to my opportunity. I did something unforgivable giving my body to another, but he made me so mad that his touch felt so satisfying. He pushed me to him I had justified but I couldn't fool myself and I hated that he made me scream his name and how I flooded the sheets with my satisfaction. Tears roll down my caramel skin joined by blood leaking from my forehead. My head throbs from the physical impact and mental wrestling I was doing.

"Are you okay?" He yells shaking me.

"I'm Fine." I answered. I saw that we were only a block away from the sound. His wheels burn rubber as he whips in the lot where I knew they were. I scream his name seeing my love bathed in his own blood knowing that he knew the truth fighting for his life. I broke out of the car and ran to his side screaming I'm so sorry! I could hear the sirens closing in on us. He coughs up blood, in excruciating pain and all I can think about is how I wronged him! Not just physically but for deeming him not a man because of his bank account like you could somehow purchase that status. I don't fight who gets to ride with him to the hospital, I know I don't deserve to be by his side after I killed him from behind.

Darruis

Sirens break the silent of the night while the rotator lights echo off the walls of the buildings. I bounce around in the back of the moving clinic with my shirt stained with blood as the road bows down to the speeding truck allowing even red lights to be treated as green. I am only a few inches away from the medic but his words ring faint and despite the expedited transport, time seems to be moving slowly.

"300 joules ready!" The medic shouts

"Ready" His EMT responds

"Clear body"

"Clear!"

His chest rises with the potential to hit the roof of the ambulance had restraints not been in place. White gauze turns into red sponges as it rest on the entrance and exit wounds. The oxygen mask appears to almost be suffocating him as hands pound on his chest cracking bones forcing life in his body.

"Stop compressions!'

"Analyzing rhythm, analyzing rhythm." the machine repeatedly says.

"Shock able rhythm detected."

Clear body!"

"Clear!"

His chest bursts up once again.

The medic gets on the radio with the hospital. "This is unit 137; I have one black male 27 years old gunshot to the abdomen, shoulder and upper chest right under the left clavicle. Pulse is faint, blood pressure is dropping. Excessive hemorrhaging. IV is already started, epinephrine already administered, shocked twice, continuing CPR. About 10 mike out how copy"

"I copy last, preparing for arrival in 10 minutes." The radio replies

Family and friends at home didn't have what he needed where we were speeding away from and the cold fact was they were the cause of his suffering. I wasn't optimistic about his recovery; I wasn't hopeful that he would pull through. I instead preyed that the lord forgives his ways and forgive my people. Death where I come from is not the beginning of a new state of existence, it's the stage of judgment where actions will be accounted for. His debt would soon be reconciled with the lord that night as his final breath was taken with a gasp. His death shook my existence and the whole community woke up through his nightmare.

Chapter 3

Darrius

My typed words are supposed to pull you into this story. It was my assignment all along it seemed when Omar came into my life. Where to begin is unknown, the story isn't even about the person fighting for his life in the ambulance, the person that pulled the trigger, the woman's actions that flooded her guilty conscience, the border line racist police officer, the death of the little girl that set the train in motion, the Islamic lady, Omar or my life for that matter. It isn't about my wife that hated me at a time, my kids who don't know me! It is defiantly not about my brothers that inhale so much weed that oxygen seems to be a pleasant surprise to their lungs. I guess in a sense we are all just pieces, and this book is about putting the puzzle together. The puzzle in essence was about entrepreneurship. Something that you learn in a business course at your local community college or buy a quick success book! I mean really, entrepreneurship caused the dramatic opening to this book! I guess if I put it that way it does appear comical but know this entrepreneurship is freedom. Freedom was change in my community that had a tradition of enslavement encompassed in a culture that upheld ignorance. You see slavery kept my community in line; it wasn't until Omar introduced us to freedom that transformed our old way of thinking. However change always has a price to be paid and sometimes the person that pays doesn't go on to enjoy the outcome, it's us the people that are left behind that usually enjoy what sacrifice brings.

Saying all this I struggle trying to put not just my story but all our stories into words. How do I tell you the reader of the cold, the fear, the struggle, the emotions, hell I even find that the biggest obstacle is the damn title for this book? The title is supposed to somehow pull you to my story and has only a few words to be deemed worthy by the reader to give it a fighting chance. My father and I had disagreements about the original title of this book "the black entrepreneur walks in you" is what I called it. "Darrius black is going to have your audience lose focus on the issues your speaking about unless they are black. You will appeal to one race and will be ignored by the others." He continued " if the power of words can move nations, create dynasties, influence a people of a higher being, establish governments, make people give their lives then what makes you think that a word can't get an audience hung up on it. The reader will see black as a title and unless his skin pigmentation matches the title then the book will be invisible to him." My father couldn't have been more right; racial identification has assembled so many exclusionary ideologies that it is a member's only kind of theme. Language is persuasive in its nature and is meant to communicate ideas that develop perspective. Due to this, one opinionated word can misrepresent the whole paragraph running the risk of misinterpretation, and one controversial view point can contaminate the whole speech making it fall on deaf ears. With that I state this. This book is not only for Black people, it's for everybody sick of trading their time for money, that can't afford them a second with their passions! This book is for everybody running on the hamster wheel of debt trying to run faster and faster only to have that wheel speed out of control! This book is meant to wake up that inner entrepreneur spirit in you. The black community has had a plague of disadvantages in the American dream and reflects in Seattle to this day, with only 1.7 percent of businesses being owned by blacks. We are at the low end of the totem pole and because of that it has introduced street life to our culture as a sense of survival that diseases our communities. This message is for everybody to wake up especially the hibernating African Americans.

Darrius Booker was the name given to me on March 14, 1989 at Swedish Hospital by my mother's mother. I was Born in Seattle one of the most prosperous cities in America but lived in Saints Grove a place avoided by others who have the funds to live beyond my neighborhood. This story didn't just arise from my imagination or fantasy. This book is in essence an open dairy of the truth about the black community. These pages captures the symbolism of all black communities by telling the story of one place called Saints Grove, WA; located in the south side of Tacoma, WA about 30 minutes without traffic from Seattle. There are many locations like mine throughout America but Saints Grove is the place I call home.

The scene is set in a place where apartments are claustrophobically crowded around one another matched with the individual units that are populated above capacity. Like the apartments, houses are in close proximity with cars spilling from the drive way into the yard with beasts barking and snapping at people walking by. The children play in the streets and scatter when cars come down the lane. The streets are lined with bared window businesses that foreigners run, drawing its financial power from every spare dollar of the people of this community. The exceptions of these business is Taylor's Soul which is a black owned restaurant with Mr. Taylor being the owner who's been around since the beginning of the town it seems A Barbershop and Baptist church, buildings down from Mr. Taylors joint. The passage of the week: Psalms 132 verse 1-3 displays on the billboard just before the church building, I always wondered how many people actually read the passage of the week as I passed by it on my way to work every day. The tour continues and if you look to your left and right you will see walls of structures are used as canvases splattered with graffiti, the beautiful building tattoos are messages to those who understand. We understand these messages of territories, landmarks, and affiliations and trend with caution pass certain parts while police patrol with suspicion. On the sidewalks vegetation grows from its cracks on the cement, littered with cigarette buds, broken bottles, swisher sweet wrappers and stained with urine and spit. The drunks, Meth heads and dealers ornament the neighborhood making the town come to life. Clouds provide a roof in the sky and you can see the breath of people waiting on the bus in the cold December climate.

The people dream of a better existence outside these blocks while others in the community infest the blocks with shadow businesses. The life of this community is further insulted by actors portraying this way of living as cool and the music industry defining it as real. Doctors, Dentist, Politicians and business owners are fantasies and dreams while dealing, assaults, gang banging, incarceration, low education and low wages are existing nightmares. Some people make it out of this neighborhood with success, the majority however only transfer between these types of places or remain captive in this area. This community is not even referred by its true name, its more common titled projects, ghettos or the hood.

The people that call the hood its home are an assortment of rich chocolate, cameral, mocha, cinnamon, and butterscotch completion. They are a people of rhythm, stylish lingo, and vibrant attitudes and personality. They do not see their environment as rich farm land waiting to be tended to produce rich fruit to enrich their land, the people here only see a land fill that needs to be cleansed. The police and land development take the job of cleaning out the hood by taking shadow business off the street and remodeling, buying out, and raising the cost of living forcing the occupants to another location turning it to a suitable living environment for the future residence.

Growing up in Saints Grove my elders always lectured that God works in mysteries ways and that it was not my purpose to understand the lord's plan but live according to his word. Even though I was coached this way I always tried to decipher God's strategic layout with so many questions arising. Why was the standard of satisfactory, lust and temptation so strong that it crushed giant like potential? Why was the flesh so weak that the slightest force could tear us apart? Why did it always seem like the black community was always aboard a sinking ship? Why do our people fail to see the value of life until the last breath is taken? It was so easy for us to turn on each other, pull one another down and decline support to our own. We only seemed to come together during tragic events. Some of my friends that passed had more people attend their funeral than their graduations, birthday parties and weddings combined. I was told that God worked in mysterious ways with a plan but I tried to understand the plan he had for the African American. Gods plan always seemed random with good deeds being met with bad consequences, Love met with heart broke, and helping others usually turned to enabling them. I have always been taught that you will reap what you sew. So, I never understood why this quilt of good deeds I sewed could never keep me warm in this cold neighborhood.

When I wasn't questioning the lord all throughout my child hood I would read books of my black ancestors fighting for freedom that we celebrate one month out of the year. I saw the faces of black crusaders on monuments, museums and TV specials from time to time, but never in the chain of command in the military. I didn't see them in the CEO category; I didn't see them in congress until Obama appeared. I looked all around me and didn't see them in many businesses. They didn't produce the car I drove, or the pan I cooked in, they didn't own the gas station I used to fill up my tank nor the bank I deposit my check in. I saw them in reality shows but knew that the owner of the network didn't come from a community like mine. I heard them on the radio but knew the owner of that industry wasn't someone who looked like me. I saw them on the shoes I wore but knew the CEO could not relate to my community beyond our spending patterns.

It would be silly to say that none of the people in my community had the capability to run corporations and conquer a market. Everybody is born with the same potential, maybe not the same resources but definitely the same potential for greatness. So why in this day in age do I find my community so far behind all other races in this race. Why do my peers believe that they are warm in this cold world with no quilt!

A string of bad luck I always assumed marking us the cursed ones. I believe the lord grew tired of my constant questioning because for one week God went to work. A meeting by chance affected me and the people closes to me. A man that goes by Omar spoke to me and his audience grew as I brought more to him. He spoke of treasure hidden inside our untapped potential which really related to me because I had always dreamed big but produced pebbles to the mountain of my aspirations.

God gave me a view of how life could be in my dreams, taught me to see the real world through experiences and built a bridge from that reality to my dreams through this man known as Omar. Omar had no last name we knew of so we couldn't link him to a family here, we didn't know the title of his employment or even when he moved into this neighborhood. My friends, family and I never seen Omar up until this point in our lives. Omar was a bald hazelnut colored 6 foot, 180 pound man, with a long beard that hid the front collar of his shirt. He always had a different variation of a black shirt with black slacks. I saw Omar continuously with his seeming to be Muslim lady assistant for one week at various locations where he would hold meetings. We used each other for our own interest, I for his words and him for my writing. Omar must have had known that his time was limited and knew that the whole black community couldn't be reached by his voice and the mind of those who heard him wouldn't portray everything he said but the words could capture his moments, his voice and his intensity in a book.

This journey is a reflection on the week that changed my life and all others who called the SG home. Fall deep in the text that follow, feel my reality as it relates to yours, find the common ground with your dreams compared to mine of a better life, and then let these words be the microphone for Omar's voice.

Chapter 4

Stone

The steam of the roosted coffee beans radiating from the cup fill my nostrils as I breathed deep. I cautiously sip the bitter black liquid harboring the taste as I let it sit in my mouth before I send it to the rest of my body. I think my body has built up such a resistance to caffeine that I don't believe it does anything for my wake up but I still have to have it. I wear the same 5 suits in a row with 20 combinations of shirts; I don't grab a brief case but a 9 millimeter Beretta and a badge that I slip on to my belt. To my family back home in the suburbs I am a hero, a warrior of justice; however the closer I get to Saints Groves the more my hero transforms into villain.

The area I am sworn to serve is the area I punish. This low economic area is home to unemployment, government dependence and single parent households as a result drugs infest these blocks creating a perfect breeding ground for gangs and violence. The population that resides here are blacks and they frequently see my vehicle as a demising site. I've been on the force for 15 years 6 of those years as a detective, I am known around these parts.

Many white folks are scared to say their opinions when it comes to race but not me. This whole black lives matter movement is the biggest joke, now I'm not saying that my brothers in blue don't do some fucked up shit but the blacks are far from innocent. I have always thought of them as cows eating beef, they eat themselves with calling themselves nigga, defacing their own property and infesting the neighborhood with all sorts of illegal activities causing their homes more pain. Do I feel bad for them, hell no! Their ancestors get my pity, but this generation feels that the world owes them something and because the pain the ancestors suffered is somehow their right to benefit from. The black card gets pulled so much that they think we should forgive them for failing to abide by the law.

I hate how sometimes the judge goes soft on some of these boys that walk in there. I'm a product of a single parent home, my father was in and out of prison all my life, I was born into poverty, you name it I have heard, but despite all that you still know right from wrong. Even though I am for bringing the law down on anybody who breaks it I also understand these streets.

Some white people even call me racist just because they have a black friend or two, but they don't live in the hood or the projects, they yell criticisms at people like me from their gated communities but want my protection when shit hits the fan. I can be the dark knight however, do the work that everyone else is scared to do and ask the questions others shy away from.

I pull up to my assigned parking lot reading detective Stone. I remember when I first received this title, how happy I was to finally make a difference. I think back to how stupid I was as well, I don't rehabilitate people, I don't provide any therapy for the perps I only haul them in and only see numbers adding to a statistic. We don't do shit but become more militarized to the communities we serve. Hell we only respond to the world around us, there is a church every other block, community centers and schools and I still find most of these hoodlums outside of these infrastructures spraying them down. I see bums sleeping outside the corner store with a hiring sign right in the window. The drug dealers that make a fortune slanging product to their own people don't reinvest it into their schools or extracurricular activities program. Instead I see rims gleaming down the street, I hear subwoofers blast nigga and bitch and I smell drunk mothers probably purchased with selling food stamps or their child support. I shake my head thinking about it as I gulp down the last of my now barely warm coffee.

I walk into the precinct seeing many familiar faces in the processing chairs. I know some offenders better than I know family members. My route to my desk gets interrupted when the chief calls a huddle in the conference room.

"Good morning everyone. As I'm sure you all have heard there was little girl shot dead in the west end of Tacoma. No eye witnesses want to step up but we found some surveillance footage from an adjacent convenience store that may have captured the suspects and their vehicle. The techs are going over it now. Stone and Cordell your up, I need you to start on this case. The mayor is all up my ass on this one and we need to solve this. Rival gangs in Saints Grove are likely the corporates behind this slaughter so I am going to need a neighborhood canvas. West Tacoma division has allowed us to do some joint task work to bring these ass holes down.

Chapter 5

Darrius

I bury my feet deep in the warm fine almost liquefied gravel, the microscopic pebbles filling the space between my toes, the smooth casual breeze makes my attire dance and directs my eyes to where the golden frosting meets the sapphire marine. My wife and kids emerge on the scene almost as if God had just illustrated them. Years prior when I was an enlisted man, I had held this whole beach in my hand on a flight to Al Dhafra Air Force base. When my squadron and I landed, I mushed the beach in between the pages of a traveler's magazine and shoved it into the seat in front of me. Now Matira Beach a small island in French Polynesia has immersed me in its paradise and all the luxuries that are served to me before I even desire them. It's funny how when your scraping your way up through your current obstacles all you can think about is that future of fulfilled wishes before you request them and once you have arrived at your aspirations all that seems to consume your mind is your past struggles and the people left trying to find their way. I think about my friends back at Saints Grove having their leash jerked, choking out there day dreams of better lives and reviving their reality with GET BACK TO WORK, WE HAVE CUSTOMERS! I think about my people dragging their minds, bodies and souls.... almost there they think, just a few more minutes until break time, lunchtime or the weekend. I think about the community that raised me that relied on temporary weekend mind numbing vacations just to make it through the upcoming week!! Oh, how I want them here with me. My life success is rare in Saints Grove and all black communities in that respect such that I am usually the only one in first class, 5 star hotels or limousine services. Only the flight attendants, house keeper of the hotel and driver of the car match my complexion and neither one of us can truly be happy for one another. I must go back and show them the way, I must go back and show them that their feet can to follow my foot prints in this warm sand I bury my feet in. I tell my family lets go back home.

As we walk I hear a faint alarm type sound in the distance. It gets louder and louder ruining natures orchestra, the waves dry up, the cool breeze turns into a hot thick comforter set dog piling on top of me. I look up at the sun and it forms 4 digits. 05:30!! Damn I'm late!!!!!

I wake up to my reality!!! I try to find motivation to jump me up to go tackle my day but for years I have not been able to locate it! I found instead fear that drives me, the fear of the first of the month, the utility bill, car note, water bill, daycare bill, student loans, money that I owe my father to pay off a wealthier collector that as they get richer with my late fees I fall further into the trenches of debt. I crawl out of my slumber and stand up out of bed fighting the weight of gravity. I walk to the bathroom passing my roommates, I love you daddy see you tomorrow. My daughter shouts with such optimism. Man, children are funny, she knows how my work schedule is she won't see me until the next morning for a few minutes before she goes to school.

I kiss my other roommate a good day, her eyes that was once filled with passion, so much passion that if you looked deep in them you see a phoenix blazing with fire all around its huge wing span banging its arms against her pupils ready to escape to conquer the world. Those eyes have sense dulled out; I don't know if it's from the fatigue of her 8-month pregnancy, her 45 hour a week job, or her motherly duties with two children after she gets off work. Due to my work schedule she takes these tasks by herself. Yes, her eyes have dulled out all right, she has nothing to look forward to today, she smiles at me and tells me to have a great day as well "I will just see you today for the ultra sound appointment!" She boasts, Damn I had completely forgot, I haven't told her that I couldn't get today off. I will let her be happy for a few hours before I call her at work on her lunch break with the news. She loves me out of obligation these days, and I commitment. The passion in our lives has been frequently denied from either mine or her employers, it's just not a good time they tell us. My roommate takes my other two down the stairs to the car.

I remember the good days I had with my wife and children before I had this job when we had lived with her mother in one room. I remember how I loved the time we spent together all while hating myself for not being able to afford a better life because I was in between jobs after I got out the military. The more time I spent with them the worse their life style became to the point when my wife and I couldn't take the kids to the store because we got tired of saying no the whole time. I had to leave my wife husbandless and my children fatherless to buy some happiness. Damn if you do damn if you don't I guess. My roommates understand, husband slash daddy must work!

I splash water on my face and rub the sand out of my eyes wondering why I came back after the military. I had escaped Saints Grove and had a pretty decent life, all I had to do to continue my life style was just sign my life to the government for another 4 years. I hated being owned however, being a patriot meant following orders I didn't understand or was privileged to know. I hated how my superiors never resembled me and thus didn't understand the struggles of people like me. I hated how they said in the military everyone had a fair shot. The only reason why the color black was so numerous in the military was because of the color of the M4's, M9's, M249's and all other weapons in our arsenal that we armed up with. I wasn't allowed to express myself to leadership, they didn't see my culture as professional. The few blacks and by a few I do mean a handful that made it to the top ranks were almost unrecognizable in character and could only be tied to me due to their physical makeup. I left my cushion house on the military base, all the amazing benefits and income stability for my freedom when my 6 year enlistment was up only to be enslaved in the job market.

My eyes focus on the reflection in the mirror, looking at the man looking back. Many times I don't recognize the stranger staring at me but not today. For some strange reason, I know the man in the mirror! The smooth almost iron pressed coffee skin carpets his chiseled cheek bones. His manicured facial hair designs his defined chin. His forehead comes to an abrupt stop as the razor straight hair forms a perfect frame. His hair is jet black with ocean waves flowing throughout his skull. As a married man it's always been hard to work alongside women's lustful attraction towards me.

The other ladies eyes pierce with envy knowing that another woman captured my heart. The diamond ring repeals my employee's advances and keeps them generating wealth. I prefer this, never mix business with pleasure is what my past master use to tell me. He was a pale wise face man with scars of fatigue around his sunken eyes and blotches of red on his cheeks. He had bleached thin stranded hair that flowed back. His wrinkled hands always use to comb his hair back when he spoke. This man had once held the keys to my chains who exploited my work allowing his family feasts and mine crumbs. I laugh at my misery back then with the humor of success. His arrogance never saw through my physical features into my sponge of a mind mopping up all his unintended teachings. This square footage use to be the plantation I was enslaved to. I agreed with him that business and pleasure in the same roof is the ingredient for failure but I couldn't pass up the opportunity to purchase this estate when it came out on the market when he went out of business. The pleasure of owning something that use to own you was defiantly my purchasing point. I have sense done some redecorating and established an empire that generates assets beyond expectation. My community loves my success not for their appreciation of my extravagant life style but the opportunity I represent to feed their desires of a better life. I sit in the office that once was the big house I looked at when I was in the field.

The water forms a pool in the sink that over flows its containment. The water fall lands on my feet knocking me out of my plush office and into my bathroom. I turn the facet off and look back at the stranger looking at me. I finish my morning duties, grab my uniform, backpack and before I could hit the door, I hear the TV on in my room. I can hear my electric bill running up as I get closer to the TV. The news is on informing the public about a shooting that took place the other night on the west side of Tacoma.

"On a cold Sunday witness say they heard shots fired at 1 in the morning shooting up the house on 5th and Washington. Officers say when they responded it was an unforgettable scene, viewers are warned that the testimony the officer gives is quite disturbing."

The camera switches to a white marine looking officer with a jar head haircut, there is not a hair on his facial as though puberty didn't come for him. I laugh as he talks about the gang violence that plagues West Tacoma and Saints Grove, thinking this is like them commercials showing starving African children. I know other people are just drinking there coffee thinking god that's awful, to us it has been the norm and a culture we embrace entertaining those around the world with our rap lyrics, music videos and movies. The officer concludes "We believe the shooting was drug and gang related targeting this area for drug territory." The camera switches back to the lead anchor.

"Task force says the shooters are still at large and urge witnesses or anybody having any information of the where about of the perpetrators to come forward to authorities, the community is to be warned that the people who suspects are to be considered deadly. The shooting claimed the life of an 11 year old girl caught in the cross fires of the turf war. Back to you Michelle." The TV goes black as I shut the power off. I shake my head with the news I received.

Niggas just don't know how to act I thought as I hit the door ready to tackle my day.

I drive away from Saints Grove's poor economy to the opportunity in Seattle. If you seek money and education you leave my zip code and head north. I'm in a rush frozen in a sea of vehicles, I-5 freeway is legendary for its put your car in park and lift the parking break traffic. I look around at my new neighbors surrounding me and know by the expressions on their face that we all have unified thinking. Where is everybody going, I have a meeting to get to, I am late for an appointment, etc. I look at sprinkles of red and blue berries flashing along the freeway, you will see one every corner the freeway turns just about. They seem like sheep herders making sure we the sheep stay the course.

I look at the police with anger sometimes, not for their periodic intrusions into my life when I'm not in compliance with the traffic laws, or even for their fame for excessive force the news broadcasts. Being a law man myself when I was in the military I understand that most of them are upright but to many of them immoral. No, I'm mad because they refused me, denied my ability, declined my experience, rejected my life I crammed in my application and resume. My 6-year military service for the United States Air Force Security Forces Squadron fell short, or my two-associate degree fell inferior; or how about my experience as a EMT saving countless lives in the back of my ambulance and those who lives dependent on that patient? I thought I had my competition blown out the water when I was sitting waiting on the police Chiefs interview with my jam-packed resume, little did I know the other recruits bonds surpassed my accomplishments, and all they needed was a fraction of my resume and some relation to the hiring committee.

If it wasn't for me not being a member of their white only club it was definitely my credit score that was my disqualifying factor. What do they expect! The banks credit cards find their way to the new young adults long before the police department and college brochures do. I hate Military and College stigma of unrealistic success. Always saying you will get a high paying career after completion, or veteran's preference, just sign your life to us here and sign over a life time of payments there!! If you look hard enough it probably says in microscopic font, with white ink on white paper not applicable to most, results vary, no refunds when results don't hold up to brochure expectations. Some side effects include but are not limited to debt increase, many classes not needed for career field but are still required, marriage will suffer due to constant absents, jobs may not be available once term is served and etc.

I'm already an addict, I'm late for school right now before I head to work. I picked up another college brochure and changed my major, I read the large glamorous black print and the small white print on white paper and am doing it again in Business administration. I mean don't get me wrong I love being an American, love the fact that I served, I feel accomplished in my studies, we American people are ten times better off than most country's but man try as I can with all my might I'm still not satisfied and desire a bigger piece of this American pie these rich folks is saying is so delicious. I hate parking at this school, can never find a spot, I must sprint to class, should have woke up earlier!

I walk into my first class on the first day of school. The room is filled with jolly young white kids that will probably hold the lives of many black men and women on their payroll. My eyes scan the room as to pick the most appropriate seat. I instantly see a stranger as everyone in the class room is at the moment. This stranger however has long braids that hangs down from her head framing her brown skin. She sits all the way in the back of the room, her eyes meet mines with a sign of relief that she will not be alone this quarter. She knows as well as I do what we expect of each other. Before I even head her direction, she takes the backpack from the seat beside her. I take my seat and we instantly fill each other in with our information. Her name is Alisha from the north end of town. Her beauty goes unnoticed in the room as the other men circle around blond and light brown haired, blue and green eyed women. Her dark brown eyes, beautiful lips and shy but confident personality immediately draw my married attention. We hope that the two of us can represent for or people in this class of 35 students. We will be each other's support system two and half hours two days' week for the next 3 months. We know all of this before the instructor even introduces himself.

School is out! I stampede along with the other students to the parking lot, jam the keys in the door throwing the bag of expensive knowledge in the back seat and pull off. I have one to two hours to battle traffic and put the armor of my corporation on to join the army of soldiers defending our brand and attacking the market! I pray that this degree will promote me through the ranks of these massive armies, hoping that the boss deems me worthy to fight for the corporation's goals. I pull off and the line of cars are halted for the crossing students without jobs. Ugh there pace is so slow, just smiling conversing with one another. These students usually have parents that blanket their lives making them warm and comfortable, what fools they are not knowing the cold world they will soon step into.

Traffic thaws out a little and allows me to arrive at work just two minutes late. I tell my car to suck it in as I squeeze in between two obese pickup trucks. "Darrius your 3 minutes late" my boss greets me at the entrance. His name is Max, a person that conforms his dreams to his employer. Manager is the best title he has gotten so far in his life and everyone working knows not to mess with his pride and joy. After Max tells me how the repercussions of me coming in late negatively impacts humanity I clock in to listen to my new bosses. I cater to countless commanders as they delegate there orders to me. Yes, sir, of course ma'am, No problem. I clear my throat as I answer to another superior. I even aid my new coworker in helping serve her bosses better. She struggles trying to match our products with their needs. Her name is Lisa and like me she is from the SG. She stands slender at four foot eight but her spirit is Goliath. Max holds the sling shot knocking her down with everything she did wrong that day. She bears the rough counseling on her performance, she knows that she will be able to vent to me later. I want so much to go toe to toe with Max on her behalf but I'm in his world and choose to act as though I didn't just hear him belittle Lisa in front of costumers. The customers love the actions of Max. When there wants aren't met promptly they enjoy seeing that action be taken upon the person not meeting their expectations. In their opinion her lack of experience in her new position is no excuse for them to be inconvenienced at our store.

I retreat to the back of the store where I score an Advil, I've been under the weather lately but I don't have time to be sick per my sick leave hours. I'm only aloud so many hours to be sick a year at this establishment so I try to space my sickness out accordingly, plus I have vacation time I have to use starting tomorrow. For one week I will have time for the things I feel is important in my life. Time speeds up as the traffic in the store increases giving me plenty of work to focus on. I give my employment all my energy until the night consumes the sky. I lock up the store already preparing my mind for tomorrow's freedom.

My roommates have already drifted into their alternate realities by the time I arrive home. I sit at the kitchen table and pull out my knowledge books to prepare for the next class day. Studying hard to earn more rank amongst my peers beating my competition out of the spot so that my family can be better off. I fall on the couch feeling defeated by my day. Funny part about it is some of my friend's mothers say "why can't you be more like Darrius" He has a job and goes to school, they leave out he never sees his kids and that his marriage is on the rocks, they only represent that I have money to pay bills.

I feel my mind racing; it can't be like this I tell myself. I walk into my room; the blanket is draped over her body. I peel the covers off and slide next to her warm body. I sync my breathing patterns with hers and time travel to the moments of happiness that seemed to follow us everywhere. We were young, our warm hearts and even hotter desires would raise the temperature in this so called cold world. Our conversations would lead us to vacations we would take, houses we would build, Children we would surround with privilege and lucrative meaningful work we would occupy. Our parents would retire and our brothers and sisters would ride the wave of our success and wash all over the community of our origins. I smile at our optimism those days. My body sinks deeper into the mattress my body relieves its fatigue, my eyes pull the curtains down and reality stops.

Chapter 6

Lashandria

My cheeks are on fire from the abrasions caused by my face sliding on the velcro like carpet as I dove down trying to escape death. I don't have time to scream, I don't have time to feel fear I only have time to shield my body from the glass that rains on me. BANG! BANG! BANG! The sounds come crashing through the windows and pierces the walls. The bullets run through the house like a rat darts across the floor. "Mommy!" my daughter screams knocking me out of my own self-preservation making me stand straight in the mist of the bullets stinging the house. I run up the stairs skipping two at a time. "Get down Ziah!" I scream through the door as I ram it down with my shoulder. She is balled up in the corner screaming hands concealing her ears. I home plate slide to her grabbing her arms jerking her back and forth, twisting her patting her down to see if any blood can be found.

My heart resumes beating when my hands come up clean from my inspection. I hold her tight like a snake would its meal crying hysterically. I hear them burn rubber on the concrete evading the consequences of their actions. Romans mom stumbles in the room half-drunk shouting are yall okay. I can't answer, my words are trapped behind the tears dripping from my face. I rock intensely back and forth feeling her little body shake against mine! His mom storms out of the room screaming into the phone "Come home now! Your fuckin friends shot up my house!"

She called Roman before the cops knowing that Roman would put us in his top priority speeding to us.

Roman

"Nigga punch that shit" I yell at Tone as the car drifts hard to the left, the back tire hitting the side walk like a speed bump as we made the right turn down my street. We drag race to the front of my garage coming inches away from knocking down the garage door. I snatch open the door and elevate out the low riding Monte Carlo, I can see the bullet holes in the window, side of the house and the door as I bust through the front entrance. I see nobody down stairs in the living room or dining room. I go towards the light in the kitchen and see my mom barely able to get any wine in her mouth with her hand shaking so much.

"Mom are you okay?"

"Get the hell off me! I told you your life would end your life and now you got your own mother, and child caught in the cross fire! Who the fuck shot up my house Roman!" Her fist start beating on my arm as I block off her attack. I grab her arms squeezing them against her body and post her on the fridge.

"Calm down mom, ima find out who did this, where is LaShandria and Ziah!"

I don't let her answer I instead sprint up stairs and break through Zaih's room. I see her squeezing Ziah rocking her back and forth.

"Babe you good? O my God tell me yall straight!" I pry her arms loose of Ziah and force myself in between them. She buries her face in my chest tears seeping through my shirt and Ziah's head goes over my shoulder leaving only her frizzy hair in my sight. I take the place of LaShandria and rock them back and forth.

I can't believe they came at me hitting my spot like this. I didn't see any turned over furniture or opened drawers so I knew it wasn't them hitting a lick or nothing. Naw this shit was personal and I knew exactly who did this. Shit if it was who I knew it was then that meant they knew it was me who hit that house! I hear Tone climbing the stairs.

"Aye my nigga is you good!" He disrespectfully shouts up the stairs as he climbs up. 2 Tone was the type that couldn't turn his nigga off, no matter the situation he only knew one kind of language to speak to someone with.

"Im straight man just dip out homie ima check ya tomorrow!"

"Man Ima find out who did this, don't worry about nothing!" He said jumping down the stairs. He knew as well as I knew who was the prime suspect. I grip my ladies tighter and rock them till we all crash beside the bed.

2 Tone

I pull out my Glock so I could sit down comfortably in my seat. I push my shit out of Romes spot and out on the open streets. I can't believe them mutha fuckes came at me like that. I see niggas can't keep their mouth shut either, so I think I will pay my homie a visit. I pass the Taylors Soul restaurant on my way to the bar seeing them through the window shaking my head as I passed by. I still remember Mr.

Taylor when we were younger preaching about having something that's yours. I snicker thinking about all the taxes he probably pay just to be broke. I bet that business is eating him up alive. Every since that KFC got strategically placed by his restaurant his business has been eaten alive by debt with no body coming in them doors. He wake up every morning to serve people that won't even give them their presents. They say I'm the stupid one for doing what I do, when I making more than anyone of these struggles niggas out here. Shit if they morals is going to make them broke then im going to do without mine to become rich, damn what the elders say. Most of the time they die broke with debt and Im suppose to take advice from them.

My thoughts pass the time as I pull up to the bar. I snatch the keys out the ignition and walk through the doors alerting everybody of my entrance with the doorbell jiggling.

"Whats up Tone." The bartender shouts from behind the bar, "what you having?"

I walk up to Michael aka Bone because he was the skinniest thing you would ever see, he was sitting next to this young curvy female that look like it was way past her bedtime on this school night.

"I figure you would be here homie, I will have what he havin!" I said landing my heads on his shoulders.

"Whats up Tone." Bone said surprised he was seeing me I guess, especially for the fact I had sought him out.

"Shit nothing, what you bout to make me drink?"

"I just order redbull and vodka"

"O shit that must be what talkin muthafuckas drink, I guess I can see that though. The red bull give you energy and keep that mouth running huh"

"Huh, look Tone I didn't say nothing about.." I punch his face to the counter making his head bounce on the wood. The female he was with started screaming "Please!"

"Shut yo ass up before I have you both leaking more than the words you already spilled."

"I'm sorry Tone please.." I whip my Glock out my waist band bringing the steel across his face splattering blood everywhere.

"I said shut the fuck up nigga! Your words got heat put on us that's not good for business! What's your position homie?"

Bone stutters trying to speak through the blood and swelling consuming his face "To to to tooo drive."

I put the barrel to his temple engraving the opening in his skin. "Exactly, so that require you to run your damn mouth."

I stand up and look around the bar waving the gun at everyone in the bar. I felt like I was conducting an orchestra the way I had everyone moving to the wave of my hand.

"That goes for everyone in this bitch. Shut yo ass up and I won't have to come in here wildin."

Feeling I had made my point I stopped pointing at everyone retreating my heat back in my person and fleeing the bar. The cold air doesn't cool me down as I step outside, I look back at the bar and then down the street smiling about the power I had. I think about Mr. Taylor requesting respect hoping people hear his words whereas for me I command it having their full attention. I remember Mr. Taylor talking to me when I was younger telling me that all money wasn't good money and that people fearing you would only give rise to a rebellion against the oppressor. Shit he couldn't have been more wrong in my opinion, the government uses fear, the justice system uses it, these corporations control their employees with fear with people hoping they don't get fired. Shit if you ask me instilling fear is how you stay competitive and whether its good or bad money you can still spend it the same so who gives a fuck. The IRS sleeps good at night snatching up these folks wages so I sleep good as well. It's the so called good people that fall asleep stressed out and there only hope for it is an afterlife that hasn't even been proven. Shit people don't find it hard to believe niggas parting the red sea but can't understand why I rather be a self-made man than a slave to this bullshit ass work system. I make money off people the same way corporations do, and that's feeding their desires, and if they could tax what I do they well probably employ muthafuckas on the corner slanging this shit.

Red and blue lights fill my rear view with a loud whoop whoop! Fuck, they aint got nothing better to do than to pull over a nigga. Happy that I didn't have nothing in the vehicle with me I pulled over with ease. I could tell by the lights and the front of the vehicle that it wasn't a regular squad car. The lights make only the figure of the body visible. I throw my heat in the middle counsel knowing they needed a warrant to search my shit. The hand knocked on my window to roll it down.

"Is there a problem officer?"

"Well if it isn't Andre Patterson." His voice sounded familiar and knew it couldn't be no one other than Stone. This punk muthafucka always had it out for me. He had put them chains on me most of the time I went in when he was a patrol cop and one time when they let his racist ass become a detective.

"If it isn't overseer Stone, making sure your niggas stay in line right?"

"More like making sure you observe the stop sign you blew past. If I could just have your license and registration I can get you on your way, I'm sure nothing will come back so this will just take a moment."

I shove my credentials in his hand knowing he was just fishing. The shooting in the west probably made me one of his prime suspects. I knew he didn't have shit on me. Moments went by when he came back with some bullshit.

"Looks like you have a bench warrant for skipping a speeding ticket, I'm going to need you to come with me."

"I didn't know you handled hall monitor shit."

"Just step out of the car slowly with your hands in the air his partner yelled." I didn't recognize his rookie he had. I could tell he was strait from the academy by the way he was patting me down.

"This is some bullshit, yall just fuckin with me, talking about some punk ass speeding ticket. What about my car?"

"Don't worry I will have a tow come pick it up, I'm sure you wouldn't want your vehicle in this neighborhood." The cold chains where in place with the clicking sound tightening down as they threw me into the back of the car. They said some bullshit about some transporting personnel on the radio and took off.

The shackles are rooted into my wrist burrowing deeper into my skin as my body applies pressure into the seat. The seats are rock cold making my ass conform to its rigid posture as I feel every pebble the car rides over. A black cage separates me from the windows as my uniform chauffer transports me to the station. I hear the officers talking about what they were going to do once there shift ended. Aint that a bitch I thought, while they hauling my black ass off they discussing what type of beer they going to drink. My life wasn't worth shit to them, and that's why their laws didn't mean a damn thing to me. They were foreigners to me, invading my land and chaining up my people from the damn reservation they put us on.

I can tell his partner was prior military because he had that same stupid Hair cut I use to see Darrius in when he visited every now and then when he was in. The car stops with my head hitting the front of the cage. Dirty muthafuckas didn't even strap a nigga in. They snatch me out the car and throw me in an emotionless four walled room with a cold steel table and three steel chairs.

"All this for a warrant for speeding huh?"

He answers me with a smirk as he shuts the door with his exit. 15 minutes seemed like an eternity in the small artic room. A tactic they used when they are trying to sweat you. I knew niggas that cracked before the first question was asked waiting for the detectives to come in. Two all American men walk in with their selves rolled up, I'm guessing showing me they meant businesses.

"Andre Patterson my longtime friend how have you been buddy?"

"About as good as you are at throwing niggas in the cage business, so in that comparison pretty damn good."

"You know Andre you have always been a funny man, convincing yourself that this department just patrols your neighborhood for no damn reason. I mean after all you and your crew that you roll with are complete upright productive citizen's right?"

"Shit I'm only being productive in the environment you allow us to live in."

"Look let's just cut the shit, I know you pulled the trigger in that shooting that slayed a little girl! You talk about me raiding your community and you're the one taking lives off the earth, black lives at that so I don't think you're in any moral position to question me, as a matter a fact the only position you need to fulfill is answering my questions."

"Your questions huh, well how about you refer all your questions to my..."

"Now before you say that Andre let me just remind you that I know you wasn't the only one, hell why should you be the only one that go down for the actions of others, I can help you but if you won't allow me to you will force me to nail you to the ground. But if you give your side of the story I'm sure we can work out a plea deal."

"First of all I don't know shit you talking about. Second don't act like you have my best interest at heart, and third you can refer all your damn questions to my lawyer!"

Stone

Andre was defiantly a product of Saints Grove, molded to be tough and jagged. His code that he lived by always baffled me in a sense that he saw me as the enemy. With no hard evidence tying him to the shooting I had no choice but to free him back into society. I will put my life on the line for the law but at the same time I hate it. To many holes for people like Andre to wiggle through; between the neighborhood not talking and the sophistication of these criminals it's likely that we bring only a small percentage of justice to the criminal world. He knows that evidence in this case is limited, that's why I'm going to enjoy wiping that damn smirk off his face when the time comes. What he doesn't understand is that it's not some black guy that was in the street world who got gunned down, this was a little black girl that the public is going to want answers and thus giving me all the power to bring results.

Chapter 7

Darrius

The sunsets over the horizon where the pacific meets the skyline, painting it in swirls of sherbet. The night follows with far fire flies lighting up the sky. My wife, children, Roman, Jeff, Shelia and Lashandra and their children halo around the blazing inferno. We gather not for the warmth but the entertainment of the dancing flames. The sand conforms to our bodies as we sit around. Laughter of pass struggles echo over the crackling of the blaze. Roman and Jeff laugh the hardest as they should with their beginnings.

Roman comes from my mother's sister and Jeff from the same womb I shared at one point. Roman lived his life in the shadows of society where he moved according to the lights of blue and red. He had a huge work place of 10 blocks that circled his address in the SG. He sold a famous unregulated product at the time that people craved more than life its self. The demand was high and supply was premium that drove the market higher than the fire flies lighting up the sky. Jeff on the other hand consumed more than he distributed and was Romans most loyal customer. There was no return policy, no complaint system, no order form for his product, and best of all no sales tax in this industry. The industry didn't establish retirement plans, 401 K, medical insurance or other standard benefits. The dollar made didn't boost the economy of the neighborhood to benefit the housing, schools and streets. Houses where still in need of repair, unemployment was still the norm, and minimum wage was the standard people strived for. This market didn't grow the economy in the SG but it did grow the economy for other business owners and government agencies like law enforcement, liquor stores, payday loan shops, and bail bond businesses. Do to the unregulated lucrative market it was common for uniform foreigners to frequently canvassed the neighborhood looking to increase the private prison system. We made more people money incarcerated then we did being free.

Churches rejected the CEO's of these product industry blaming the vary money producing market on the low quality of living in the community and the fireworks that seem to light up the night on a daily basis. Lives were never given meaning with this way of life only numbers for statistics. This way of life never produced revenue for black owned business only money for the morgue. The Roman empire was shut down due to heavy inspector audits raiding his warehouses and charging his employees and clients alike. That time was long ago as Roman and Jeff turned their back on the dynasty. Transferring their sales and consumer buying patterns into a regulated market were state and IRS were included in the running of their establishments. Their ventures in to the legitimate world turned out to be just as profitable as the shadow business.

We lay around till the swaying yellow is reduce to a red glow among the charcoal wood. The children found their dreams laying in the laps of their parents and the grownups meet each other's eyes.

"Man I never thought the fam would be here on the beaches of Hawaii." Says Roman breaking the silence.

Jeff opens his mouth and he lets out a piercing siren blowing out the barely surviving red glow in the wood, the fire flies scatter and the world disappears as my eye lids open. 05:30.

I snooze the alarm on my phone and see the date. I always forget to cancel my alarm on my day off. I lay in the bed and my agenda runs through my mind like a movie. I agreed to meet up with Jeff today to help him pass a test he wasn't prepared for. 5:30 turns to two in the afternoon as I pull up to a white 2015 Camry. The rims dipped in silver complemented with midnight windows blocking the light from exploring the interior. I take the keys out the ignition and open the door and walk to his driver's side. I'm met with fog as the window retreats into the door. Our hands meet as my brother greets me.

"What's up nigga."

"What's up bro" I shot back.

I walk around and slipped into the car. The interior of the car was to envy as we drove away from my 2002 Chevy Cobalt. The bass ruined any possible conversation we could have had as the vibration of the woofers raddled my ear drums. We pulled up to his apartment complex. The new edition cars seemed out of place in the run down apartments. The chrome rims light up the pavement as I looked down the parking lot. We exit out of the 5 star Camry and Jeff leads me up the stairs to the cheap hotel like apartment. My eyes immediately target the corner of the apartment unit where a coach that we had jumped on throughout our child hood rest.

"I see mom gave you the coach huh." I said snapping out of my memory.

"Yea bruh, she got some new shit so I copped it from her for 50." He said as he tossed the empty bottle at me. "Fill that up about ¾'s of the way, I gotta go take that test in 2 hours." I took three steps from the living room to the bathroom and felt relieved as I filled the bottle with what I had been holding for 45 minutes on way to meet him.

"How much is this new job paying you bro." I asked as we traded places from the bathroom to the living room.

"17 dollas an hour full time my nigga." He explained. In Louisiana where I came from being stationed at Barksdale Air Force Base 17 dollars an hour could earn you a decent life style in a higher quality apartment. In SG low quality housing 17 dollars an hour would grant you breathing room in paying the high rent in his same unit.

"Where's Shelia and Jeremiah." I asked looking at the pictures of my brother, his girlfriend and their baby on the wall.

"She at her sista's house waiting on me to scoop her up, she our baby sister when she go to work."

A lot had changed since I got back from the military. The boy I had left was still in high school fighting for his C average and his attendance record. That was seven years ago and now I was talking to a grown man with a family of his own. I looked at a shelf with about 6 months' worth of rent in shoes.

"I see you scored those new J's." I said sarcastically. Jeff had still owed me money I lent him numerous of times, but in my mind, I had just given it to him feeling better if I thought of it as a donation rather than an investment. I waited another 20 minutes before we headed out the door to his appointment.

The cloudy day consumed the sky as we pulled up to the clinic office. We walked through the doors and took our place among the other black people that filled the room all here for the same reason I'm assuming. I wondered if they had help passing this test. My brother waited in line while I took a seat in the waiting room. The options of seating arrangements were between an open seat by a Carmel complexion woman engulfed in her phone with her child coloring on the waiting magazines or a seemed to be upper middle aged mocha man with an army hat on dressed in all black. I felt I related more to the gentleman than the woman. He smiled at me as I took my place. The people in the waiting room was engulfed in their hand, nobody noticed the child coloring on everything.

The seat was more comfortable than I expected as I sunk into the cushion. The seat reminded me of my Eames Aluminum Group Executive Chai, that was premium leather seeming to be hand crafted for my body. 1800 dollars for this chair is what was charged to my company's expense, more than the majority of peoples pay check, I was sitting on somebodies rent. Nature met technology on my dark oak wood desk supporting my 42-inch Dell computer monitor. In front of the desk were two premium lounge chairs perfect for entertaining clients with spread sheets and proposals.

My co-worker knocked once on my door and entered, her skin was milk chocolate with glasses that exploited her beautiful dark brown eyes. Her hair had a volume curls accompanied by her friendly spirit that would have gotten her any secretary job but her knowledge, degrees and professional demeanor landed her my accountant position. She spoke in a deep raspy seasoned man's voice. "Waiting on somebody?" The people in the room had reduced and the minute hand on the clock above the check in desk moved forward 25 minutes.

"My brother" I replied.

"It looked like you were in deep thought" said the man with a smirk. I smiled back

"Naw just day dreaming, Thank you for your service by the way." I had always made it appoint to show gratitude for the people who served before me.

"Thank you brother, I say the majority of African Americans have been brain washed to settle for acceptable and deny the exceptional." I looked at him, baffled by his random response; I took the message he gave to me with a slight head nod.

"What branch did you serve in?" the man requested.

"The Air Force. How did you know I was in the military?" I replied.

"Usually a man thanks another about something he was either apart of or knows something about, by your posture I just made an educated guess I suppose. But the hat on my head is used to keep my head warm, not a symbol of service. I tell you what Airman come to my church tonight at 7, I will be speaking on how to change your life and the lives of the people in your community." He gave me his card with the address on it, I was puzzled, a few short dialogue responses and he invited me to a church, and better yet there was more than 15 other black people in the waiting room before I entered.

"Sure sir." I said hesitantly. I always had a problem with saying no. "Can I ask you a question?" I said with a skeptic look.

"If you want to know the answer" he replied.

"Why didn't you invite anybody else in the waiting room." He looked at me as if I had asked him something inappropriate and then laughed.

"Because you were exploring other realities in your mind while the others were consumed in their phones." He left me with that response saying his time was up, and walked out of the waiting room area.

Jeff appeared not long after saying come on.

"Good lookin my nigga, what you bout to get into now?" He said feeling relieved I guess that it was over.

"No problem bro, and I don't know I think I will hang around here for a bit, I guess I will link up with Roman." I said.

"Yo did you hear about fam house being shot up."

"What!? Naw when did this happen?"

"Last night nigga, everybody cool and all but I know that auntie trippin on him. This nigga aint been moved back in wit his moms for a sec and already got her joint sprayed. well shit I gotta go scoop up Shelia so ima just drop you off at your whip." I nodded at his proposal, the mission was completed, I will be on standby for the next favor he needs. We pulled up to my car and I changed from his passenger to the driver of my less extravagant vehicle.

I had a few hours until 7 so I called Roman. My eyes were on the lookout for the cops, waiting on Roman to answer the call. In the SG, they need only the slightest reason to pull you over. "Whats good fam!" he exclaimed almost as if he greeted me in person after a long while. "Whats up man, I'm on your end of town just seein if you busy."

"Naw Bruh just at my plugs house, where you tryna link up at?" He replied

"I guess your house, I'm close by."

"Aight bet."

His house was the same house we had growing up when we used to spend the night. He had the same room he had back in middle school days. He pulled up a few minutes after I did, exiting his car retrieving his backpack from the back seat; a backpack I would never let him ride with in my car. 2 Tone was riding shot gun, while Lashandria rode backseat. She brushed pass me with a blunt hello. I could tell they had been arguing with her expedited walk into the house.

"Wats good fam, wat brings you on this side of town." Roman said

"Just had to run an errand with Jeff, wats up with Lashandria?" I inquired

"Nigga she always on the same ol shit, she stays beefin." 2 Tone interjected.

"Is aunt Kelsey home?" I asked

"Naw mom at work, come on I just picked up a bottle." Roman announced presenting an unopened bottle of Hennessey.

"Bruh I heard yo spot got shot at last night."

"Man yea them bitch ass niggas from the west side of Tacoma came through blasten. Don't even worry about that tho me and Tone about to give them an early 4th of July."

"I'm just glad didn't nobody get hurt." When I said that Roman glared at me with a grim expression. With that Roman led us into his house. As we walked up the driveway I could see three bullet holes on the garage door. How lucky that those bullets didn't go up to the next floor I thought.

As we entered the house Roman immediately positioned himself in the living room and began pouring the spirits out amongst him and Tone. Roman needed to always be at a certain level of intoxication. Sober was a state he tried to avoid at all cost, when he dealt with life's normal activities. We sat a chilled until the hour hand was in front of the minute hand at the thirty mark.

Lashandra had locked herself upstairs in the room my entire stay. She always seems to isolate herself from reality. As an adolescent, she had long for adventure outside her born into community. Dreams drove her desire as she crawled her way through high school applying to the big leagues of college. Lust hid behind the mask of love as she threw herself at Roman at the time. Back then her desires to leave the SG was pushed out to make room for the new life growing inside her belly. The love for her child to have her real father made her stay to make it work with Roman but the hatred of her life styled force her to leave emotionally from him. The woman I first met when Roman first introduced us was long gone. She believed she could change him, upgrade him, and show him a new way of life. While trying to draw out his potential she went into overdraft with her own and was now forced to pay her debt to society by working at minimum wage jobs to scrape a standard life style together. The old man I had met at the clinic words rung throughout my mind *"The majority of African Americans have been brain washed to settle for acceptable and deny the exceptional."*

I looked over at 2 Tone who had taken his sober state into a coma laid up on the coach. His origins was rigid from the start it seemed.

2 Tone was born André Patterson and from ignorance. His reality is what many people portray in music videos and movies. His father was a slave to the prison for his whole life and his mother a slave to her two jobs to make ends meat. In his mother's constant absents due to chasing stability his teachers were seasoned OGs in the game and his environment harsh. Brutal lessons were learned young, no mother to cry to no father to protect him except for his only older sister named Michelle.

André wore the same clothes many times in a row to school. As kids, we could count his outfits for the whole school year usually being no more than 8 articles of clothing. 1 pair of shoes, 3 shirts, 3 jeans and one sweatshirt. Andre's hair resembled Velcro never brushed. His hands were always ashy as though he used chalk daily. His beauty and kind personality was concealed by his low material privilege. Michelle was 5 years older than André and cared for him better than many adults for their own children and was the complete opposite of her brother. Her beauty defeated their economic state. Her natural glamour and even then, well-defined body made all look past her actual attire. Her appearance allowed others to give her a chance where her personality would mesmerize them. She was the jewel of the school in those days. Kids would always tease André about being adopted because there was no way Michelle and André shared the same womb. There eggs were fertilized by different men causing them to grow apart. Michelle's father was present always picking her up on the weekends leaving André to care for himself during their mother's weekend shift.

We all grew up together Roman, André and I along with all the other neighborhood kids in the SG. I remember asking my mother if André could come over for dinner or spend the night after a long day of running around. She would allow many to stay over but never André. She would always say I don't want you hanging around him. My mother's views were shared by many always denying him entry into stable environments. André would always hear of the fun times at birthdays and sleep overs during school.

André found friends in Roman and I due to our common interest in karate movies. I will always remember the look on André's face when our mothers would call us in for dinner. His face would grow depressed as he knew what awaited him at his residence.

Over the years we grew together until one eventful summer in 2003. Michelle 16 at the time snuck out to go to a house party. A man from another neighbor not too far from ours found his interest in her. Her young heart was no match for his mature charm causing her to fall deep in love. Loving the man however came with loving his thug life style. A disagreement between him and another dealer ruined the party she had crept to. This feud turn deadly when the other dealer opened fire in the middle of the house. The crowd scattered breaking through the house running for their lives. Police sirens filled the air and blood carpeted the floor. The ambulance pronounces 4 victim's dead on arrival that night. The man that stole Michelle's heart, 2 bystanders that had nothing to do with the dispute and Michelle herself. Her death rocked the foundation of the community but even worse crushed whatever mercy and hope André had left in his life.

It seemed André made a deal with the devil that summer because overnight it seemed he turned into one of the toughest thugs in Tacoma. His untamed coarse hair was now perfectly edged and in perfect form. His body seemed to have been dipped in art, tattoos conquering his whole body. His few outfits turned into clothes never being worn more than once it seemed. His shoe string budget turned into drinks for everybody and I will take care of the bill money.

His rivalries either turned to alliances or closed casket funerals. He was to the streets as Tarzan was to the jungle. Roman was a shadow in the shadow business but André was the body that cast the shadow taking it with him where ever he went. There were two options if you were doing business with him, working for him created wealth and all you heard was dollar signs Ku Ching or become a victim by him for standing in his way or refusing his offer, Bang bang. These two tones where the only ones he offered and thus landed him his name 2 Tone. Roman and 2 Tone had become almost Siamese twins by the time I got back from the military. Together they ran a pretty lucrative empire from their mother's homes. Roman was the business man or dealer in the terms of the streets and Roman the supplier or in street terms the plug. I always wondered what could have been for my cousin and childhood friend had my mother had let André spend the night or if André and Roman had their fathers in their lives. Or maybe if their mothers hadn't been devoting every spare moment of their time chasing every spare penny of overtime had to offer them leaving not a spared moment for Roman and Andre.

I looked at the time again; the minute hand took the lead of the hour hand at the 45 mark. 15 minutes to get there I thought. Roman was high off his liquid spirits and looked up at me as I started to grab my coat to head out the door.

"where you going fam" he interrogated.

"I told this man I met at the clinic that I was going to go to his church."

Roman laughed, "Nigga since when is you spiritual, shit the preacher hustle more than I do. At least I sell niggas something tangible, all they sell you is dreams, shit that you can't get."

I looked at him with nothing to say. How could he blast the church like that, surely he knows that we receive blessings every day we wake up in the morning. "Man you going to hell talking crazy like that." I defended.

"Yea okay, I'm the devil because I'm stating facts huh. Tell me something choir boy I know you see niggas receiving awards and cats on TV talking that God shit but explain this, we grew up in the church, right?"

I nodded being careful not to be agreeable with what he was about to say next.

"Koo so tell me, you didn't see nobody you went to church with on some successful shit, your moms didn't get money, as a matter a fact she still relies on this crocked ass government to take care of her and she aint never missed her 10 percent payment to the church. Or how bout Deacon Raymond who died broke as hell, or them young girls who all ended up pregnant by multiple niggas and in the systems handout programs. Say what you want but you know as well as I do that they live check to check like the rest of us, but I tell you one thing the Pastor stayed dipped. Man, I tell you what go to that same church we grew up in and see if you don't see the same cats in the same position."

I hated the undeniable facts, faith is what drives everybody I know to make it through another day and yet he had an ugly point.

"I tell you what ima go to this bullshit wit you just to show you wats up and bet that plate going to be passed around in full affect, I'm leavin my shit at home cause I be damned if I shoot them 10 percent." Roman said putting his wallet on the counter.

"You see that's why your ass need to stop drinking talkin all that reckless nonsense." I said as we left out the door.

2 Tone was still knocked out when we left. I never understood how he trusted him to stay in the house with his woman, Andre I could understand but never 2 Tone.

Me and Roman piled into my car, I plugged the address into my phone and we took off. Down the street it displayed. Roman stayed hydrating from his flask the whole ride there. We pulled up to a two-story house, where cars were lined up outside.

"Man he invited you to a startup church." He laughed. "Yea you defiantly finna be one of his start up investors to get this shit off the ground. Man I know you know this that old house where that musilim lady used to live with all them kids." He continued. I started to regret keeping my word to the old man but I couldn't pass it up and further prove Romans point.

We walked up the screeching wooden stairs to the white screen door, before I could knock the door swung open.

"Assalaamu Alaikum Brutha Darrius you just in time, O and I see you brought company." Exclaimed an elder woman. I couldn't believe this lady still lived here and was even more confused of why this man would have church at an Islamic house.

Roman burst out laughing, "O this church must be desperate teaming up wit the bean pie community!" I could had punched Roman in the face for his blatant disrespect. I knew I shouldn't have allowed him to come, the liquor made his words uncensored. I opened my mouth but was interrupted by the elder lady "Everybody is family here brutha." She warmly answered.

She leads us down a narrow hall and into the living room, where miss match furniture formed a circle around the old Man. The Muslim lady showed us to our seats. There were 10 people in the room, young, old, different religions, some African some African American a complete mix of people. The old man looked at me with a smile. He began abruptly with a thunderous voice!

Chapter 8

Omar

WAKE UP!! His voice roared causing silence among his company.

Living in the direction of a trajectory fired from a brother that doesn't appreciate the value of life, bringing vampires to life with blood thirst, specializing in street pharmaceuticals, transporting poisonous product to your community and trading in your freedom for a cage. The street mentality has done our community no service. We are founders of illegal dynasties and only qualify for minimum wage jobs. This life style has gone main stream in the music industry world and have further injected nigga in America's blood stream. Words of unity are generated to empower one group of African Americans and push the other ones down. We constantly form gangs to combat other gangs but both parties fall victim to the police army. We as a community indulge in this street reality and wonder why we are not taken seriously in the corporate and political world. We fall victim to incarceration statistics and complain about the prison systems. We blame poverty for our situation and lack of resources. We blame the hunger of a child that made you rob a bank.

The audience nods while amen and preach on brother are shouted out.

The life of crime has never paid off and has only lead to further ruin. We look at the image this life style produces, a false reality where women are stripped of their business suites and into thongs. Men are surrounded by multiple women as if one women couldn't satisfy one man. Money thrown around like leaves in the wind as if that money couldn't be used to further our black communities. Getting multiple women pregnant, and buying things to appear wealthy without actual ownership has become the norm. We are a product of our environment. Other cultures see our reality as a fad and continue with their privilege lives while our community lives out the nightmare. Almost all gang members and drug dealers have vocalized the harm of this life style and yet the youth continue to emulate it. Why? Maybe because that is the best song on the radio, or it makes the best shows and movies that we surround our self in every day. Many black children hear nigga 100 times more then they here doctor, preacher, student, father, brother and man. Many black women here bitch 100 times more than they here, ma'am, Mrs. And lady.

These are the images that we are encapsulated in! We are branded with unprofessionalism, profanity, and womanizing vulgar language and we are the first that comes to mind when you hear welfare, single parent house hold and incarceration. It's not only the outside world that marks us with these titles! Most of the time we mark ourselves with these labels. We proudly amplify degrading lyrics about our race aloud in our vehicles for everyone to hear. We proudly upload revealing photos of ourselves to these social media sites, displaying gang symbols, flicking off the camera and our women exposing their bodies to cyber strangers! Have we come to accept this norm of Black culture? Is this the image we want our legacy to hold? I'm willing to bet my bottom dollar that the rappers of music videos would not want their daughter dancing on their music videos. I am *willing to wager that lady entertainers wouldn't want their sons referring to their wives as bitches, having multiple mothers of children and frequently being unfaithful to their women. A drug dealer doesn't want their children selling drugs. The very people that perform these activities do not deem it suitable for their own children and yet they represent themselves to other children in that fashion.*

Roman looked at the old man unconvinced. He whispered to me "man I could have waited till Easter Sunday to hear all this."

The old man turned and locked his eyes on Roman

And you! O yea you are the tool that society uses to halt progression! Yea you live in shadows afraid during the day light scared that others may shine there light on you exposing your life's work. Your presents alone invites the stereotype of a counterproductive black person or for short, nigga! However, even though you play the role of a destructive tool you can be the instrument that brings everyone in this community together.

Ramon shot out of his seat in protest!

"Me! Grandpa let's get this shit straight you up here saying the same shit I have heard all my life! People like you say only God can judge but then your hypocritical ass come at me all judgmental thinking you know everything. You got these folks eating the bull shit you spittin. You think niggas is lookin out for one another out here! Its hot out here, cats lookin to take me for all I got, it's my so called bruthas that snitch on me to 50, it's my bruthas shooting at me, it's my sistas that run they mouth talkin all that shit behind my back, the sistas that mess around with my homies when I'm gone! And when a nigga come to prey it's the church that give me the eye when I walk into the building! Preachers give me a 2-minute prayer and think that's supposed to solve shit. My kids still hungry, my bruthas still try to take me out, and my sistas stay plottin on me! When we leave this place nothing changes, just the time in the day we wasted listening to niggas like you and hoping for shit to change asking the lord to change our realities! But I'm to blame for the world I was born in! Hell if anything you old cats set the rhythm for the younger generation so I guess yall to blame for bringing us in this messed up world. Up here blaming me for a mess that was created long before my generation. You people judge me for choosing to survive instead of starve. I try working a full-time job and the IRS folks eat all my check before my babies get they meal but I'm to blame right! Look yall can dream, have these little gathering everyday but I tell you what, when you wake up and when the meeting ends yall will still be in the same spot! Yall think yall going somewhere! Yall running on a treadmill and every time you get faster to run off, society just turn up the speed taking more of yall energy!"

The room grew still, I looked at my cousin not being able apologize for his words due to the fact his words surprisingly moved me.

Brutha look at you. My words were not meant to insult you, they were meant to inform you. Your inner pain has replaced your love for your people. Your brothers are your enemy and your sisters are your down fall. You believe that exploiting others before they exploit you is survival. You've become the predator to your own people. Your very status in life invites your enemies. Your so-called dynasty is only going to lead you back into slavery brutha. You are feared by your community and have thus forced them to fight you instead of support you. You are not an infection brutha but a cure if you choose to be. You think that just because God has put obstacles in your life that he has turned his back on you. You have forgotten what prayer is. Prayer is only encouragement to do better, prayer without action falls on deaf ears even to the one above. Brutha if you can find a way to create wealth in the dark of society then you can find a way to build an asset that can be celebrated in the light of day. Feed your community opportunity instead of poison, don't turn your back on your sisters because you came from your mother a sista and have produced daughter a sista with another woman who loves you also a sista. Your sisters give you life, enhance your life and will continue to breed your blood line. Be the tool your black community needs you to be to build up its foundation instead of being the tool used by society to break it down. Brutha we don't own nothing in this land that our ancestors have built, we don't own no capital that has been gained by our labor, life is the only thing we own and the last thing we need is for it to be taken away by our own hands.

For the next 30 minutes Omar had filled the place with knowledge, encouragement and promise of better things to come. His words were like wind moving the sea of people in the room.

The liquor had washed down from Romans eyes. His whole philosophy he used to justify his actions had been taken away with a few words. His head began to look at the floor but was blocked by the Muslim woman's hands.

"We were born black before we accepted Christ or followed the teachings of prophet Mohammad, We were born black before we took an oath to a gang or to this country. We all represent different parts of society and all have individual sins and obstacles but we all share a common problem and that is unity between our people. Omar and I walk two different paths going the same direction and we need not to shame one another but help one another get to a better place. Hold your head up young man and know that it is never too late to do better and be better" She said with the warmest motherly voice

Roman saw the intensity in her eyes and knew it was the look a mother has for her children, a woman he had never known had comforted him more than his biological mother ever did. Roman took back his seat as the meeting progressed. Omar expressed not only words of hope but ways to put our actions into affect. I could see the people was internalizing every word that was spilling from his mouth. My hand filled pages of my note book capturing his words. I never understood my fascination with taking notes, most of the time I never referred back to them but I knew I had to paint this moment with words.

The night fell to 9 as the meeting came to an end. Roman who had soley come for the purpose of debunking this man soon found himself at the edge of his seat. We began walking out towards the car when the musilim woman blocked our exit "we will see you in church tomorrow brutha." She said whipping the tears from his face.

"Yes ma'am" Roman replied.

"I am not your superior, you have enough of them in your life so there is no need for ma'am, I am your sister, I want you to bring your wives or women of your lives tomorrow you hear." She said looking at both of us.

"Yes sister." We replied.

Just before Roman and I headed to the car Omar called me to the side.

"Darrius let me borrow your attention for just a few seconds. I won't keep him much longer Roman." He explained

Roman still speechless walked to the car. "Darrius your lesson is more extensive than the rest, you have homework." He said smiling

"I don't understand Mr. Omar why do you feel I need extra lessons, do you feel that your not getting through to me on the first night?"

"It's the exact opposite Darrius, I believe I have sparked your interest like no other, these assignments Darrius will make your senses exploit the black communities weaknesses. You will bear witness to your own struggles and past failures. These lessons will channel your vivid drifting mind to focus on how to make your dreams of black triumph come true. Success alone doesn't drive you Darrius, the flourishment of others around you drives you. I saw you take down my messages and you must not only write about these meetings but what you see around you."

Still confused I stated "Why do you need me to write down everything."

"You've always questioned me and now I will show you in time,"

"But I've never questioned you" I said.

"You do it every time your mind wonders about why things happen that seem to hold our people down. Your first assignement is to write both from your own life and what I will be speaking on tomorrow. I will give you the topic now: *The African American family in the general sense has been taken from our reality and repositioned in our dreams only to be woken up by society to the reality.*" Just as he had done at the clinic he left me taking the last word.

The night grew nearly to the next day before I got home. My mind was flooded by the lesson which seemed to be a statement. What did his quote even mean? My roommate was fast asleep when I arrived. I took my place beside her and replayed my day until I fell asleep.

Chapter 9

Roman

Damn I can't sleep and I am sober as hell. That whole speech had killed my buzz and mind set. I couldn't say that this was the first time I heard my way of living wasn't conducive to the neighborhood but I had always discovered loop holes in their argument giving me some type of justification. Not this time, his words bounced around in my mind and due to my non-intoxicated state, it forced me to focus on his message. Darrius had just dropped me off and I climbed up the stairs my mind flashing back when the bullets invaded my house. I couldn't help but blame myself for that, I knew why them niggas hit me. I can't say I blame them either but I didn't know that girl was in the house, it was supposed to be the plug's spot full of them street soldiers is what Tone had said.

I walk through the house immediately spotting the vacant couch Tone had laid on, someone must had picked him up I thought. My feet make the stairs sing as I climb them, I crack open my daughter's door sneaking a peak seeing her deep in her blissful sleep. The image of her bleeding with holes in her body because of some stupid shit I had done flashes in my mind. I shake my head trying to rid the footage out of my mind but the consequences my actions could had caused my family are too real to ignore.

I close my daughter's door to go to the next room over and lightly knock on my mother's room to see if she is awake. I see her in a drunken coma with the wine bottle just about gone. I know it's not to celebrate nothing, it's just to cope with my ass being here and causing all this extra drama. I can't help but think how things would be different if I could rewind time, I would be a square like Darrius and provide the legitimate way. Shit Darrius doesn't have the ideal life I want either, He barely even see his kids working like a slave but at least he doesn't have to worry about the bullets. Then again, he served all that time in the military and is right back here in the SG where you can catch a bullet doing anything. Damn is there any logic to this, 2 Tone grew up messed up, I had a descent child hood but got mixed up in this life and Darrius served his country, and got his college degrees and we are all still in the same pot. I parachute the covers over my mom's body, grab the wine bottle and tuck her in. I close her door as gently as I had opened it to keep her induced.

I entertain the devil on my shoulder advising me to down the bottle of Moscato. I lift the bottle to my lips tasting the drops on the rim but stopped before I elevated the bottle to consume. I can't I thought, I put the bottle on the night stand in my room and lie down. I can hear the shower going in the bathroom and assume its LaShandra. It's kind of late for her to be showering, I pay it no mind thinking she probably in one of her moods again. She loved taking a shower and listening to heart break songs. I guess the shower set the scene for her, I don't hear any music though, I leave the case open not caring to understand why she takes late bathing sessions now. Shit I don't have a right to ask her why she do anything the way shit has been going.

If I'm to be honest with myself I told her I am sorry about a million times. She is mad because of the danger we were in, my life has never came at her like that night but her dissatisfaction with me started way before my house got tagged up. I still remember staying up late at night with her after she had unmounted me after her climax. She would push her bare breast on my chest and roll over to her side making us look in each other's eyes. She would then just talk about her dreams of graduating college, what business she would start and where the best location to build our house would be. She would say career fields I would be perfect in and how once she got into her career she would send me off to school. I use to just smile and nod my head knowing damn well I wasn't interested in those text books. Those were her dreams mine were simply to see hers come true. I pushed the block giving her any finances she needed. My method of retrieving money was no secret to her, but in her eyes it was a necessary evil to get to the overall good. One of our passionate nights created life and one of my mischief nights caught up with me when she gave birth to my daughter with me behind bars. That was the first time I ever said sorry to her as she let go of her dreams to work a dead-end job living with my mother trying to support our child. When I got out I had to work a job as part of my probation severely limiting my income. I know she felt foolish for placing her trust in my ability to be her security, I know she had felt stupid for sacrificing her self, taking a chance on a man like me. My mind goes numb wrestling with the weight of my guilt until I pass out on the bed.

Lashandria

The room is white with fog as the steamy hot water fires from the shower head on my body. The flash backs of last night run threw my head as the water runs down my hair streaming down my curves. I pull the lofa from the shower carton and massage the soap through the flaps creating clouds in my hand that I cover my body with. The white foam smells of lavender and vanilla but even this sweet aroma cant wash away the foulness. I rinse the suds off hoping that it takes my sins with them. I turn off the water and climb out the shower to the window covered in warm frost. I whip my hand across the mirror to see my reflection still holds my sins. How did this happen, how could I have been so fragile to the temptation. The anger I had for Roman was now redirected at me.

I use to pride myself on being the realist person I knew, never scared to tell someone the truth. What happens when the truth is too strong for you to bear the consequences. Am I supposed to sacrifice myself for morals that won't help in my dealings with the penalty? My actions would only misinterpret my feelings for Roman. He won't believe that I still love him more than anything in this world. He will see my act as a betrayal when in actuality I would take a bullet for him. I can hear him snoring on the bed outside the door. I wrap the towel around my air dried body and walk out. The warm room still feels cold compared to the sauna I just walked out of.

There he is body fused with the bed. Where he lays is where I was exhausted and worked out. The pillow his head lays on is where I screamed and moaned as he speared me from behind. The covers that he wraps himself in was the same covers that cocooned us both together. I can feel my self-getting wet contemplating the kama sutra positions we explored. The way he grabbed me controlling the direction of my head using my hair for reins God I hate what he made me say, I told him it was his and that he was the best. Tears surge out my eyes joining the wetness my body produced. I hated that I wanted more, how could I be so foul.

I dry every part of me and slip into bed next to him. His body feels foreign to mine as I try to get comfortable next to him. My eyes grow heavy with my mind wrestling with the guilt.

2 Tone

The red cherry gets closer to my lips as I take a long drag from the blunt, clouds filling my body as I take the smoke deep in my lunges. The fog comes rushing out as I give myself an overcast crowding the car with white haze.

"Pass that shit nigga."

I steal another hit before I give him his turn. The sob woofers sends bass through my body as Mac Dre plays. I lay back in the seat reclined almost as far as it can go watching the sky move. I shut my eyes thinking about my dick stroking her pussy down making his woman say it's mine! Roman is my mans though and I aint got nothing against him and will fade a nigga if he step to close to him but shit the way she walked pass me I couldn't resist. Shit he didn't pay her no attention so why should I feel bad because I did his job for him.

The moment I asked her what was on her mind she just kept pouring out words on top of words telling me every feeling she had. In return I gave her every feeling she needed. She knew what she was doing coming down stairs in them high ass shorts. Her body filled her spaghetti strap tank top with her ass pressing firmly against the fabric of those running shorts. Her skin had fresh lotion on making her glow in the light. She was getting some water when I had woke up to find Roman and Darruis gone. She had asked me if I knew where they had went and I had no clue to give her.

I had asked her how she was coping with the danger she was in; she was hesitant to talk at first probably because in her mind I was partially the cause of it but my persistence got it out of her. I told her to sit next to me and to let it out. The more the words flowed out her mouth the more tears had poured from her eyes as her re-captioned of the night made her relive it. She didn't need my words to comfort her only an ear she could put her words in, I wrapped my body around hers holding her tight as she cried on my shoulders to secure her, her arms followed shortly embracing my body. Her hands grabbed a fist full of the back of my shirt with her head in my shoulders and ear by my lips. I spoke gentle in her ear of how I was going to make sure them niggas would never be back and reassured here that her safety would never be compromised as long as breath filled my lungs. She had taken her head and looked up at me, our faces inches apart and eyes locked on each other, Her breath warmed my lips with each breath and with each inhale and exhale her soft warm breast pressed against my chest feeling her nipples through our clothes.

"Aye bruh I forgot to tell you we got the spot of one of the shooters, His baby momma wit one of the homies and she got to talkin about how she cant stand how her baby daddy be causing trouble and shit. She described his latest stunt which is identical to what hit Romes spot. Stupid nigga running his mouth to a female." Drone says knocking me out of my thoughts.

"Shit it must be that niggas plan to get murked out here. Its been barely 24 hours and he already blastin about his role. I swear niggas is dumb." I say laughing already plotting how to return the favor.

Chapter 10

Stone

"All these damn people crammed into that little ass block and nobody see shit of value in this case!"

I yell as I run into another dead end.

"No luck with James huh" Cordell ask across the desk.

"Nah he has a solid alibi." I look around the prescient for any black cops that may be around before I speak my true feelings to Cordell. I lean closer to his desk.

"You know what bugs me Cordell, is how these spooks get so upset with the word nigga that they use all the time to reference anybody of importance to them but get mad when another race uses it or better yet scream all day about how black lives matter but no one in the god damn neighborhood even comes forward with any information about the death of this little black girl. I mean they have a little church sermon for her, sing amazing grace and then that's it? How is it that me, the white cop, kicking up more dirt than the black folks of this community. Black folks gossip all the time and I know somebody knows something."

"Look man you keep talking like that and one of these liberals or blacks hear you then the next time a black perp gets a paper cut in your custody you're going down for a hate crime and excessive force."

I shake my head realizing he couldn't have been more right. I lean back in the chair when I hear Cordell phone ring. I lean in to ease drop on his phone call. I can't make out what the other person on the line is saying but Cordell facial expression tells me that we are receiving good news.

"What?" I asked as he hangs up the phone.

"You know that video camera in front of the corner store that captured a car speeding away from the crime scene?"

"Yes and?"

"And that crappy ass surveillance system may not be that crappy after all. The footage was able to make out a license plate."

"Great we just have to run and…."

"Already ahead of you, the car came back registered to a Mrs. Claudine baker."

"Wait, no no I know Mrs. Claudine baker and she a 56 years old lady that goes to that church by Taylors Soul."

"Yes but did you know that she has her nephew staying with her named Michael Fisher aka Bone!"

My heart jumps out my chest, finally a lead I can go off by. I knew Bone going way back to my patrol days picking him up for minor offense the biggest one being a riding in a stolen car which got reduced to joy riding. Murder however was a big jump for him which lead me to believe he wasn't alone and I knew I could break him for information.

"Okay what are we waiting for looks like the lord threw us a bone."

"Yeah just stick to your day job comedian." Cordell laughed as we jetted out the door.

As part of Bones probation back when he got out in 2012 he had to maintain a job. A well known mechanic at Davis Auto named Jimmy had gotten Bone on part time. Bone skills were undeniable as his prior knowledge of stereo equipment and the electronics of the vehicle probably from stealing them all the time had gave him a reputation of the beats man around town. Everybody in town knew that if they wanted their stereo hooked up Bone would be there guy. It's sad how Bone never used his talent for a legitimate business. With a business plan he could had opened up his own shop and made killing out here. The streets grip on many of these black kids is so strong that it overrides gifts that can get them out the hood and transform them into curses that keep them in the hood.

Bones usual hours were from 12 to 7pm at the shop. We pulled up to all the banging and drilling of metal, when Cordell and I stepped out the car and closed the door the mechanical sounds had paused. Davis happened to be outside when we pulled up.

"Hey Stone what brings you down here, All the parts we use are all legitimate."

"I'm not here for your parts Davis, I'm here to speak to one of your employees."

"Let me guess you want Bone huh? You know I told Jimmy when he brought him here he would be trouble."

"Trouble? The word around town is that Bone has been the reason your business has been booming. I see you have been doing quite well." looking at the Mercedes parked in front of Davis office.

"Well with hard work and loyalty to the community it repays handsomely."

"Well Davis I believe your confusing loyalty with exploiting. Hiring gifted mechanics and paying them shit because you can because hey where is a black felon going to get a job at, and charging these people payment plans for your services and then stack on so much interest that they would be better off getting a loan from a bank to pay because hey where else are these people going to go, you have a monopoly here. Now I would love to tell you more about your unethical behavior but I'm on a time crunch so if you would be so kind as to get Michael that would be great."

Davis mouth dropped with no words to combat mine. Many of these white folks and foreigners speak negatively all day about the Negros but drain them for every penny. Hell I guess I'm in the same boat, my record breaking case closures was due to the blacks, committing crimes and leaving a cookie trail to the criminal. Taxes get raised to fund the jails I put them in, the food stamps they consume and all other sorts of benefits' they get then they turn right around and spend the funds at these white own establishments that fill the pockets of the owners and throws its employee's scraps. I never questioned why the blacks despised other races, everyone else builds empires to feed their families for generations while generations of them are on government assistance. I understand the anger but you don't cheat the system, you don't rob, steal, deal, and kill and justify your actions playing the black card of victimization. In my eyes once you broke the law you have become the predator.

Bone was no exception to the rule. Davis had fetched the bone over to me by the car.

"Mr. Michael how is it going, I don't know if you remember me, my name is."

"Yea Stone I know."

"So, your memory is good well this is a face you may not know detective."

"Ross, I know him to."

"I'm sorry you must have me mistaken for another."

"No, I'm sure I don't have you mistaken…"

"Look it's not important my name is Detective Cordell and this is Detective Stone and we have some questions regarding the shooting which killed a little girl, since you have such a good memory you should be able to tell me where you was on the morning off November 28th."

"Man why yall sweetin me for, yall always fuckn wit me. Im trying to do right but…"

I didn't have time for his bullshit and decided to throw the evidence in front of his face

"Please spare me the victim everybody is picking on me bullshit. We got your aunts car at the scene driving away. Now I haven't contacted your aunt to see if she had been doing any joy riding because odds are it was you." I drilled

"Man that could be anybody's car. You know how many niggas in the hood got a ford explorer?"

"Not many people with license plate AD145375. Look so far you are the only person we can pin this shit on. The Chief is up my ass to get somebody responsible. The community wants blood Michael and if you don't start dropping names and hand over the murder weapon then I will unleash every detective tactic, every English word in the reports, and all my energy to bring the entire weight of this crime on your shoulders."

Bone wasn't built like 2 Tone, the consequences of his actions was too great for his character to carry. Bone had just enough street cred to give himself a hard time finding a job but not enough to afford him respect in the penitentiary. I could see his forehead acquiring sweat, and his eyes becoming misty. A part of me felt sorry, just another kid that gotten swept up in this hood shit. There was no way his timid self could have pulled the trigger. I had defiantly found my driver but I still needed my shooters.

"Look I was out that night driving, but I didn't shoot anybody. I can't talk to yall out here. I will meet yall out back away from here at the next alley. Is that koo?"

"You got 15 minutes to tell Davis whatever in the hell you got to and I will meet you in the alley. You better not be bullshitting me Bone because I will spare no expense on your ass if you try and play me."

"Okay. I will meet yall there."

Cordell and I headed back to the car, I was finally excited that this case may be able to be closed. I knew I could flip Bone for all that he had.

"Hey partner I got to go take piss right quick I will be back." Cordell said.

"Just do it behind the car."

"Look Stone you may have no standards for privacy but I do. I will meet in the alley." Cordell said disappearing into the bushes.

I crank the car and pulled into the street right into the alley way. I turned on the radio to hear the same old 10 songs they seem to put on rotation.

Bone

"Look you better have not brought no shit into my place of business Bone! You are a good radio man but I can find others to replace you that cause far less trouble." Davis said spitting when he talked.

"Chill out Mr. Davis I will be right back I just got to go holla at them for a few, I will be right back." I said unsure of the future that awaited me.

The heat was getting hot and I immediately regretted my big ass mouth. Tone was already on my ass when he stepped to me in the bar and if word got out that I was choppin it up with the police then I was good as dead. I walk out of Mr. Davis office and head towards the alley, in an instant I regretted stepping outside in this thin ass sweater. I hit the cross walk button so that I could shoot over to the alley pulling my hat down so I wouldn't be recognized.

A familiar voice yells "What up snitch ass nigga!"

I turn my head looking towards the street. The 2004 Camry creeps in front of me with a man dressed in all black with a black ski mask. He is holding a 9mm Uzi hanging out the passenger side window, I see the muzzle flash and feel the heat in my shoulder, chest, stomach, neck, both thighs and the right side of my rib cage as bullets invade my body. It's funny, I thought there would be more pain as I feel myself get riddled with bullets. This must be shock, it has to be. I hit the pavement hard with my head bouncing on the rock surface. I hear the car speed off and can hear people screaming. The ground is so cold and I can feel each breeze throughout my body.

Fuck how did I get myself into this, I know who did this, my own fuckin crew. Hell I can't even get mad, I was just about to turn them in to save my own ass, there is no honor amongst thieves. Every bad decision I ever made is just flowing through my mind, every regret, hell I don't even know if I can get right with God at this point. I knew that me talking would have consequences but I didn't know it would come so soon. I didn't even say shit yet. My vision is getting blurry and I can feel myself drifting away almost like I'm going to sleep. I know this isn't something I can wake up from, the burning sensation in my body feels too real to be a dream. Blood pools in my throat and I find it harder to breath. I can feel my chest taking in air.

I look up and see Detective Ross or Cordell by my side, he doesn't say hang in there or nothing, he just looks at me. I drift in and out of consciousness but I can piece together him saying shots fired on his radio, but there is no sense of urgency in his voice. I know he had something to do with this, I want so badly to reach up, put my hands around his neck and choke the life out of him but I'm choking my damn self on my own blood. I can't say what's on my mind, I can't believe this is how it's going to end. I'm going to die feeling so cold, so cold that I feel like I'm lying naked in the street. I know I'm not going to be remembered, I have no legacy nor did I ever get a chance to plant my seed. Fuck man my auntie, what about my auntie! Damn I'm not ready to go please! Damn the shit is getting dark, my time has run out, God please have mercy on me!

Stone

I break every traffic law to get across the street back to where I was. I park wildly in the front of Davis Shop and jump out of the car with my gun drawn aiming the barrel at everyone. I see the worst news I could have possibly seen today, Bone gunned down. Cordell is frantically trying to give him CPR, I rush over to them yelling.

"What happened!"

"I don't know some guys jumped out of a camry and started lighting the block up."

"This doesn't make any sense, how did they know to hit bone, we just got a hit earlier today? Where were you?"

"I was taking a piss and then I heard the gun shots, I ran out to the front and I see Bone out here shot up."

"So which way did they head?"

"I don't know it all happened so fast."

"But you just said you saw that the vehicle was a camry so how are you not going to see their traveling direction?"

"Yea, yea it's all coming back to me now. They made a left on Jackson street."

In the heat of the moment you can forget details and most of the time memories start running back to you once the smoke clears but there was something about Cordell I didn't trust, something in my gut. And if you're a detective you never ignore your hunger to be noisy. Bone had called him Ross, and the look in his eyes when Cordell corrected him was one of confusion. Bones untimely death to coincide with Cordells bathroom break was too much of a coincidence.

"Fuck! call EMS out here and lets cordon this area off and get a blanket over Michael so he isn't being displayed out here. This is the last thing we needed! Our only Lead!" I yell jamming my gun back into my holster.

Chapter 11

Darrius

The wind is warm and moist. The trees and plants look as if they had just been freshly planted. Flowers fill in the forest with vibrant colors while birds produce nature's symphony ringing throughout nature. The trail leads us to an opening where water cascades into a body of water made of white crystals as the lake matches the brightness of the sun shimmering in the day. Roman, Lashandria, Jeff, Shelia, Mike, Tasha, my wife and I look around at the portrait view produced by the 2-mile hike through the Costa Rica Forest. We all smile at our ladies; this is just not a hike to some pretty view but a symbol of our journey through trials and tribulations to our paradise of love. Each couple holds their mate for their own reasons but nobody holds each other harder than Mike and Tasha. Mike and Tasha had been friends turned into lovers during our enlistment in the military, and I had seen them blossom from acquaintances to holy matrimony.

Tasha was fire that could ignite in a moment that attracted everybody with her warmth, and the fire that set her passion ablaze with her man during the midnight hour. Mike on the other hand was gasoline that set everyone around him on fire with his charisma and character. Mike never new a woman to deny him and Tasha never knew a man to turn a blind eye in her direction. The inevitable meeting of these two would combust into an ecstasy fueled by bliss and rage.

There titles for one another turned into shackles forbidding them from any external person. There disagreements turned into violent wars. Caring actions turned into revenge plots on one another. Mike and Tasha's strong love and attraction for one another had transformed into an addiction of obsession. The military couldn't contain the fire thus causing their chain of command to release them prematurely; their parents couldn't put out the flames that engulfed them causing their guardians to stop supporting their relationship. Once completely in the cold world their flames burned out of control to the point of destruction until fire created life.

The child inherited her mother's eyes and her father's dark mocha skin. Mike and Tasha created life that consumed all hearts but Tasha fire spirit and Mike gasoline character would only burn any trees planted by them so the spilt was just as inevitable as them meeting each other the first time.

In the forest in Costa Rica however they stand consuming each other in their arms. Two beauties creating a beautiful relationship. My wife turns my head to her face, she looks me in my eye and says wake up, wake up, wake up. My wife turns into my roommate waking me up to get the kids ready. My roommate is the spitting image of the wife of my dreams physically but emotional she is far from her as she could possibly be.

"Babe I need you to get the kids ready, I'm running late for work." She said rushing struggling to put a shirt over her and my son in her belly.

"Aight," I said waking up "O and by the way I need you to go to this church with me today when you get off."

"Since when do you go to church?" She said with a confused face.

"Well it's not really church, it's a……… well you will just see when we get there?" I said not quite knowing how to fully explain the environment Roman and I had experience the night before.

"Okay babe, just make sure the kids are on time for school." She said rushing a kiss and rushing out the door. I turn on the TV and the news immediately grasps my attention. I turn up the volume to hear the report.

Yesterday Saints Grove has had yet another shooting in broad daylight claiming the life of a young man. Rachel Kim is at the scene with more input, Rachel.

Thanks Shawn, yesterday the streets of Saints Grove was terrorized when a drive by shooting turned this troubled community into a war zone claiming the life of Michael Fisher while he was standing in front of his place of employment at Davis auto. Michael Fisher was a native of this community and his death has put two this week with the first being the young child who was caught in the cross fire a few days prior. Police are considering the possibilities of the murders to be linked together. Officials are urging the public to come forward with any information regarding the murders this week. Shawn back to you.

I couldn't believe Bone had died, I mean he wasn't an angel and he sold a little weed here and there but he mostly did his stereo hook up thing. He wasn't in nothing to where somebody would order a hit out, that's just not the way he rolled. With him being a known affiliate with 2 Tone I couldn't see anybody bold enough to just take him out. First Roman house being blasted then Bone being gunned down meant that this had to be some kind of turf war. If that was the reason for all the bullets then there would surely be more bloodshed. The body count rising in this neighborhood wasn't surprising as it was disappointing. It seemed all that was required for you to be a victim of the hood was to be somehow connected to it whether you were an active participant in the criminal world, a resident, or a little girl.

I walk over to my little roommate's room; they were sound asleep. I wonder if they dream of costa Rica and vacation beaches as well. I impersonate the alarm clock that wakes me up for work in the morning. The kids resist the wake-up call turning over and pulling the covers up. I smile at them reminding me of Jeff and I when our father did the same thing when he woke us up. I snatch the covers off them and they scream "mommy please!" Their eyes cleared up the vision from their dreams to the sight of reality and saw that it is me awaking them. Their eyes widen screaming daddy! My presents have always seemed to be a surprise to them despite sharing the same residence. My work schedule has always contradicted quality time with them. Chasing money for the all the things they could possibly ever want in life has alienated me from what they really need.

I escorted them to the bath tub; I know that my roommate always bathes before there slumber but I repeat this for the fact that only I do the car wash routine with them. I cater to their imaginations simulating the sounds of the car wash and making them shiny knew. I fill their little stomachs with cereal and get them dressed. I portray a tailor acting like I'm measuring their arms and legs and step back looking at their closet with my hand on my chin thinking aloud, "which outfit will be perfect." They love this even though I have already picked out their outfits before they woke. I chauffer them to their schools and they leave me saying daddy I love you! I laugh, they act like they had just came from an amusement park with their excited good byes. I think all the time I should allow them to skip school so I could spend my last few days off with them, but school is what they need at this point. I turn to my empty car and pull away.

My pocket vibrates, "Hello"

"What's up!" she responds. Without even looking at my phone for caller recognition I already know the person on the other end.

"What's good Tasha! How you been, I just had a dream about you and mike" I said laughing

"Well I hope you dreamed us apart because I'm done with Mike! He is the most selfish man on this earth!"

Depending on the day you I would speak to Tasha he could be her knight in shining armor or the dragon trying to devour her. I would usually meet up with Tasha to calm her down or arrange a meeting point for Mike and Tasha but that was during my enlistment. We are 2650 miles apart these days. Her and Mike live in Georgia and I in Washington. Believing that this was another one of their low points in the roller coaster I attempted to coach her saying that it will get better just as a rollercoaster goes back up. This was different however, her voice was stern, her words were serious, and worst her demeanor seemed calm. These traits are of a woman fed up with something.

"What happened?" I asked

"He left, he left his wife and child to go do whatever the hell he does! He only sees his desires and puts me and his child as a second priority! I know it's another female!"

I know by the time I hear from Tasha the problem has been redundant. She seems well researched knowing the divorce process, child support and custody regulations. Her words shouldn't surprise me, anybody that knew their relationship viewed it always on edge on an unstable platform, and yet I was still caught off guard. They usually always work it out in the end.

"Let's just calm down and give this decision sometime before you go full throttle with the divorce. How did this happen I talked to you guys a week ago?" I pleaded.

"He mad because we don't have our own place and he tired of living with my parents, but I'm like dude we have to do this to stack money to get our own spot. We can't be like we use to because we got a baby now, with no base housing and low paying jobs. We need to stay with my parents!"

Their relationship was fragile from the start, the independence the military provided made their love blossom but the sudden exit to the civilian world and entrance into her parent's domain suffocated the delicate flower to the point where the roots died. Mike was always a free spirit and needed his own space where he has dominance over. This type of space required finances, both something they did not have. Due to their passion for one another their flame spread out of control during one of their heated arguments causing the military to discharge them early. Mike wanted out of the relationship while Tasha wanted desperately for their family to stay together. Mike needed time alone away from Tasha, and as time and space between them grew their fire for one another burned less. Tasha feels another woman is the candle to Mike's new flame and she wanted Mike to suffer.

"I just can't no more Darrius, I just can't! I want to see him go through it, I want him to feel the pain I feel, I want him to hurt how I hurt! He plays with my heart like you would any toy and when he's through he just throws me to the side. I didn't get married just to get divorce Darrius! I gave up my life for him! My career, I went against my family and worst of all I brought life into this toxic environment!! I trusted him Darrius I trusted him!" Her words were interrupt by her cries.

Tasha

He's voice goes mute after I finish sending my feeling through my wireless network. I never understood what these men wanted from women. We give and we give all of us only to find out we would never be enough to satisfy greed. Men want complete dominance, success, and sexual satisfaction and one person was never meant to be all that. I spill my feelings to Darrius not because I admire him as a committed husband and role model for men but because I can trust him. Many of Mike's friends attempted to utilize my pain for access into my bed, every man in my life outside of relation and Darrius found my distress so sexy. That's not to say that Darrius didn't find others to take advantage of, but he never messed with his home boys ladies.

Darrius was a man I frequently confided in and many times envied his wife thinking how lucky she was. Its comical because Darrius found his head in others that wasn't what he married. His personality was flirtatious in nature and being in the military only manifested that trait into full blown adultery. Darrius was a different kind of low done bastard back then, he many times wanted that woman he was stroking to be Chelsea becuase there constant feuding didn't allow any room for passion. As the arguments grew so did the gap that separated them making every temptation and inevitable sin.

Mike on the other hand was addicted to the chase and different variety of pleasure. No matter how good the loving was it would never be enough to quench his thirst. Back then I couldn't believe that I wasn't enough for a man. My loving couldn't be imitated, my personality couldn't be replicated, the way I made his toes curled couldn't be mimicked but that couldn't had been further from the truth. The truth is all your rights eventually don't matter because all the wrongs becomes the focus; all another woman has to be is right in your wrong. A lesson like this could only be taught with heartbreak in my case and as cruel as devoting your whole life to a man only to find out that you wasted life is, it was a humbling experience. Mike had a bottomless appetite but Darrius was looking for something that was once had but was lost.

Darrius was a man that could be redeemed and a person that I wanted so much for Mike to be. In my opinion all men have slipped in another whether they admit it or not but I could tell by Darrius absent response that he couldn't vouch for Mike anymore the way he used to. Darrius couldn't tell me to move on from his friend because he knew he needed me but couldn't tell me to stay either because he knew that I was already at Mike's dead end. My baby breaks the silence with her crying bringing me back to the reality at hand.

Darrius

I opened my mouth to speak words to Tasha but her words weighed heavy on my heart. There was nothing I could say to make things better. Another baby momma baby daddy was beginning and their child wasn't even 3 months old yet. This situation always seemed to be the norm in my generation. Omar's assignment struck inside my head. Just a coincidence his topic went hand in hand with Mike and Tasha's situation I thought.

I could hear the baby crying in the back ground when I was on the phone with Tasha. "I gotta go Darrius if you talk to Mike let him know I'm done with his ass." With that the phone disconnected.

I thought about Mike and Tasha as I pulled up to my favorite coffee house. It was owned by an Italian family that sold over price coffee drinks but hey it was the only one in Saints Grove. A tall caramel latte, no foam, with two pumps of vanilla whip cream to top it off was my usual. I sat enjoying my dose of caffeine thinking about how Mike could do this to Tasha. Another woman capturing Mike's heart was not out of the norm, I to fell victim to lust in my marriage and barely survived. My wife still audits my phone from time to time but I closed that adultery book long ago. As much as I wanted to think of Mikes actions as foul I saw a lot of myself in him. His game was a sport I played many times before. I use to actually justify my actions, thinking if a woman doesn't keep my attention that meant breach of contract and that I could go with another woman at my will. My thoughts of Mike and Tasha transformed into my own relationship with my roommate Chelsea.

I remember when Chelsea turned from an embracing the world girl to a fighting the world woman. My actions contributed to this. She was the girl in high school with a light that stood out in a sea of shinning diamonds. She was fooled as many young pretty ladies are in their adolescent years that their prestige in high school would carry them through out this cut throat world. I was considered a miss match at the time with my shy demeanor and low profile social life compared to her almost celebrity status. Every dog has its day is a true statement as I grew into myself my first year in college becoming the type of person that looked down on my passed self; giving me the false view from the attention of others that blinded me from what was real. We took vows of holy matrimony after I dropped out of college to join the military. Her star high school resume was not transferable to the outside world; she became my side kick and followed me as I went hard in my military career. She stayed trapped with our first child in a four-walled apartment while I traveled the world. Making my low enlistment salary didn't allow her to venture out to school and go to the workforce because we couldn't afford childcare. She stayed home attending to our daughter. Years went by as I completed my enlistment accompanied by a few associate degrees and a few encounters with other women I had gained on the way. She acquired an empty resume, a blank college transcript, another baby and an insecurity for any woman that looked my way.

I treated her like a product that could be substituted by numerous options. I took care of her financially and she should be grateful was the mentality I had. My oppression on her caused rebellion and thus caused tension that further pushed me to others. Our arguments made it easy to confide in other women, to indulge in their temporary satisfactions. She symbolized many black women that sit in the stands amongst other spectators watching their men play the field. They get no recognition when they get the rewards. Many times, their met with the man's regret for even being involved with them in the first place. Black women are too many times titled the producers of offspring instead of the givers of life, teachers of the future and supporting the soon to be strong men and women that will accomplish amazing feats in the future.

I hate that she had been reduced from my wife to a roommate who I barely saw. I once again placed her second. I worked nonstop in the military taking classes on the side so that I could climb my career ladder forbidding her a spare moment because that was time wasted not making money. What is worse is that I justify building someone else's asset with my labor instead of building up our marriage for her wellbeing. The owners and CEO's of these corporations establish wealth for their wives, children and family while mines receive financial frustration from the low wages we bring back along with the stress of work we bring home. The irony is I had to leave all my problems outside of the door before I begin working for my boss and then pick up the same problem outside the door after I clock out an bring it to my home! I never thought of having money work for me so that I may spend more time with my wife and children. I didn't even dream of attempting to get out of this time for money making everyone else rich system to establish my own asset to afford me a better quality of life, both for money and time. Yet here I was like most black families in Saints Grove that will probably die without even trying to build capital.

I followed in my parent's foot steps to provide for my children. My father worked for many companies and my mother was a faithful servant to the City in her employment working for Seattle. My brothers and I would wait for our parents to be released from their employment to come home to us. We sprinted to the door when we heard that door handle turn. There warm faces would greet us with temporary enthusiasm before the fatigue from their work day set in. Our two-parent house hold transformed into a single parent dwelling as we grew older. Although we had two rooms, two houses, two kitchen tables, two birthday celebrations and just about two of everything our real total was half of one. When we had a mother, we had no father when we had a father we had no mother. This style of living was the norm in America especially in Saints Grove. The mother is burden with performing two positions, and in rare times the father carries the weight of two positions. Many of my friends had many temporary substitutions as their parents tried to find new companions. Although the emotional burden of a parents absents contributes to a huge factor in many black kids lives the financial strain of a single parent hits even harder. All my friends including my brothers and I had parents that labored for other people for money. Due to the responsibility of providing our parents had to work longer hours and many times hold more than one job. Our parents kept up with the bills in exchange for them being absent in our homes.

Our actions from our younger years where isolated from our parents due to their attention to their employment. The absents of guidance became the main ingredient to our delinquent teen titles. Classes were skipped, drugs were experimented with, gangs were joined, and children produced children. We saw our parents slave for others and thus created an ambition for us to either work for a bigger boss making a better wage or fall victim to the shadow business. Some of our parents indulged in the dark world and landed them behind bars completely away from their children and others relied on hand outs given to them by the government. We grew up to either manipulate the welfare system, work in the criminal world or get a nine to five. Entrepreneurship was never even considered as we didn't see our kind in those positions. Our role models where athletes, rappers and movie stars never CEO's or business owners. We saw our own community as a purgatory going nowhere. We dreamed off leaving our neighborhoods to the more established white communities. We grew tired of us robbing, killing and destroying each other. We wanted to live in the private school residences.

I followed my parent's footsteps. I came from a sheep that produced more sheep. Omar's words rung throughout my mind until the lesson became clear. I took out my pen, pad and took a shot of my caffeine. Chelsea, Mike, Tasha and my parents all went off in my mind simultaneously. What was the black family doing! I looked out the window and happen to see a stray dog walking around the parking lot and then Omar's assignment set my hand off spilling words on the page.

I wrote: *I am a wolf. I was always a wolf. Our ancestors that were first brought to America were wolves but slave owners knew of our strong nature and was the reason why they would slay our Alphas, divided our packs and injected in our brains that we are sheep meant to be herded for their use. We had to dress in sheep costumes for survival because submitting was the only way your life would be spared while resisting might as well had been suicide. Somewhere down the line however we forgot we were wolves and believed we were actually sheep. The sheep is mind numb following where ever the herder directs them but a wolf is a member of a fearless pack, an aggressive pack, a pack ready to conquer territories. The wolves travel together and hunt together forming a strong force. Sheep are easily dispersed when frighten. We only recognize we are wolves when we are battling one another. We fight as lone individuals instead of as a pack. There was a time when the sheep costume served as a survival tool but now that same tool that kept our ancestors alive is the same one we use to keep us only surviving never conquering. A pup needed their parents to teach them like the kids on my block. The mothers purpose was to birth and care for their young ones not stay* away and the Male wolf was meant to lead the unit not leave. My father was an Alpha, my mother a fearless wolf and thus produced more wolves, we only forgot what nature created us as. The black family needed to go through this wilderness as a pack if we were to do more than just survive but establish our territory.

My hand went cramp jamming the pen on the paper. I picked up my paper headed home to get the sleep my wife woke me out off.

Later that day my wife got off. Her huge belly had made her feet swollen from standing and she plunged onto the couch. I had already picked up the kids and dropped them off at her mother's house so we could prepare to go church.

I greeted her with a passionate kiss. "I love you baby" I said giving her mouth back.

Her eyes grew with curiosity, "what has gotten you into today?"

"Just been doing some reflecting today, are you ready to go?'

I can tell by her face that she regretted agreeing to go. Her long work days made it to where all she wanted to do was relax. She takes a deep breath "Yes babe lets go get this over with." She tiredly said.

Chelsea

My feet are throbbing in my shoes and every part of my body is exhausted ready to retire for the day. I really didn't feel like attending any social event especially one to hear another speak. I wish I knew then where my weary level would be because I definitely would have denied my attendance.

The look on his face holds persuasion convincing me to ignore my fatigue. His eyes always had that same convincing look even when I knew he was lying. He had given me every reason to take the kids and leave him back in the day. His tense words, desperate pleas, and mesmerizing stare, would most of the time over shadow his lies, threats, demining comments, and adultery acts. It got to a low point where his skeletons would all come pouring out the closet and I would blame myself for opening up the closet door.

I always said I wouldn't be one of those foolish girls that allowed men to treat any sort of way and yet love has a way of making all who defy it look stupid. Many times women don't understand the hold the other has on their heart, the lust, good times, and physical satisfaction entertains us while cupid tights those chains around us. By the time an unforgivable event happens to us we find ourselves stuck in our mind while our emotions and heart blindly take back. I had chained Darrius to my own identity and couldn't go back to the drawing board or starting over with another.

Darrius was the love of my life turned source of my pain. His actions made me so paranoid that every look in his direction had a sinister plot behind it. Being played turned me into a player myself when I used all his hurt to justify feeling good with another. I did it just how I did with Darrius even better in many cases. Unfaithful quest however is an addictive rush, it either craves your guilt or gets you caught in the high of the forbidden fruit.

We have learned to live with our actions because once you step out in a marriage you can never go back to the place you were. We build up the new place we are at now and hope that it cannot be just as good as the place we left but better so that we may never be tempted to step out again. I say yes to show support and he is asking me to go to show I'm his one and only. I don't fight him and allow my love for him to overpower my desire to stay home.

The place he calls church however is far from the vision I had in mind. The two story house barely looks like it should hold a family much less a group of people worshipping. When you think of Seattle you don't think of Saints Grove and when you think of church you don't think of this residence. The mask of appreciate for bringing me went on my face as we pulled up to the curb behind a red Honda Accord to park.

Darrius

I immediately noticed Romans car when we pulled up to the house. I helped my wife climb the wooden stairs and just as I had expected the Muslim woman opens the door almost as if she had anticipated our arrival at that moment. "Assalam Alekium brother Darrius, and this is" she inquired

"Chelsea his wife" she declared filling in the puzzle.

"So nice to meet you, you will really enjoy today's meeting" she said leading us into the house and to the circle of furniture. Roman and LaShandria had already taken their seats. We exchanged greetings and prepared for another night.

Omar comes from the back of the house and enters in the middle of the now twice the size population and takes a bite out of an apple. He places the bitten apple on the ground and began as he had done the previous night with a thunderous.

Chapter 12

Omar

WAKE UP! BLACK FAMILIES Wake up

Our worst nightmare is the world we live in. We live in a world where relationships change with the seasons, Love is used for temporary purposes. Marriages are contractual agreements, two parents in the same household are jaw dropping surprises, two people loving each other for 50 plus years is considered old school because that don't happen these days. Baby mommas is used more than mother of children and respectable women; Baby daddy is used if used at all in some cases due to the absents of fathers instead of leaders of the house hold and protector of family.

The audience nodded in agreement. Each couple looking at one another.

To many times black men are hungry and take a bite and leave the rest. That same man when he is hungry again will take that same piece of food and expect it to taste just as good as the first bite but time takes away from its freshness when exposed.

Omar picked up the Apple he took a bite out of and we all could see that it had started to turn brown.

Many men will indulge in a woman when she hasn't been with another and open her up to love. She wants to be consumed in her mate. If a man consumes her she will provide him with nutrients, satisfy his hunger and provide him with substances. But to many times a man will just take a bite and either expect her to be identical to the women he left, but the time after he didn't consume her she has become sour and non-tasteful to the man. other times, men will just take a bite or two out of many apples turning many rotten for the next.

Some women on the other hand expect men to deal in there decaying state. They have fallen from the tree and have been turned brown and shriveled and expect to be sought after like the reddest Apple high in the tree. If you want a man worthy, then allow him to climb high for you. Don't hang from the low branch when anybody walking can just jump up and grab you. If you require little effort to get than that person will do little to keep you.

A man that is hungry enough with aspirations of the best quality will climb to receive you. When he does get you provide him with the freshest taste and fulfillment. A good man with good taste will not go for rotten apples and an apple with grand quality will only draw the man that's wiling to get you and consume you whole.

Black sistas you need to be that juicy apple at the top of the tree and black bruthas we need to be willing to be the man that will climb up that tree and receive it. Do not be greedy bruthas and try to grab every piece available. God made these ladies to satisfy you for a life time if you consume all of them and not just take a bite and leave. Ladies when that man gets you, you be all that he needs so that he doesn't go hungry. But it takes both a non-greedy hungry determined man and a fulfilling high placed apple to make that possible.

But it goes deeper than that! The tree its self must have strong roots that blossom so that it may bare good fruit! The *branches must be strong to hold the apples in place and tall enough for men to climb. Mothers must be this tree and produce strong daughters to be that high apple. Mothers must lead by example and fathers must see their daughters as the top of the line.*

Fathers must plant the seed in a place where she can be shinned upon, in soil that she can dig her roots in and water her with fulfillment. If men tend to their trees they will be strong for him. Fathers must be present to care for the tree and teach their sons to climb high to receive their substance and consume them whole.

Bruthas and Sistas if that cycled continued we would have a forest of strong trees, a flood of red delicious apples and a slew of full men

Rotten apples exist because men leave them to spoil or the women put their branch to low, hungry men exist because they never consume the whole woman or they take a bite out of multiple women at a time never becoming full.

We can wake up from this nightmare!!! Time to fix things is what we all need; however, time alone makes no impact unless you have resources to back it. We need time for our men, women, sons and daughters but time isn't free as a matter a fact it's very expensive! Man and a woman cannot enjoy the comforts of each other if the switch turns at work or deplete all their energy to the point where all the home becomes is a sleeping station. Parents cannot be there for their children if their work schedule denies them availability. I understand money is a necessity to live however we should not live to work we should have our work fulfill our lives.

Yesterday I spoke on the crime and illegal businesses that dominate Saints Grove and many black communities in America and I am now speaking on the black families. Building assets and community businesses replaces shadow businesses, the money benefits the community and building businesses and investing allows our money to work for us so that with our new found time we can work to rebuild the African American family.

We must take our money and invest in our own communities because without the money to pay the price of time we will never be able to afforded time for our families that desperately need it. The current trend in Saints Grove is that men and women part from each other and parents from their children to work for someone that doesn't care about their community nor the responsibilities at home they must bear. What do they say? Leave your problems at the door, have your husband, wife, mother, father, kids work around their schedule!!! But how do you leave your marriage issues at the door, how do you have your child's life a 2nd priority to an employment that probably doesn't know your child's name. To add salt to the wound that employer doesn't pay you what your worth! You work building some else's dream while you go broke, you provide the owners family grand vacations and quality family time mean while you can't remember the last time you spent time with your children or your spouse. You must request time to take off for your anniversary, or see your sons football game, that or schedule your annual love and son's passion around your employer. How will the men find time to teach our sons to climb high for that apple or how will the women be able to grow their tree if we are too busy planting others.

We have planted and grown America since the beginning of this country and I for one feel its way past time that we start growing our own crop so that our sons will have opportunity so that they won't have to turn to the shadow business and our families have the time to be a family. WAKE UP!!!

Hair stood up on my goose bump skin, my body temperature had heated with my palms so wet that the pen I was holding slipped out my fingers, I launched up knocking the novel I had written from Omar's speech out of my lap screaming yes! I had never been so moved, motivated and inspired in my life. I was joined by everyone else as we moved the very foundation of the house with our approval, everyone one standing up clapping and shouting Amen! Even Chelsea found the strength to jump up. Roman in particular was really applauding, his whole life he tried to make sense of the world and take advantage of what scrapes he felt society had left for him when all along his was standing on fertile ground. LaShandria was beside him cheering wildly. Every eye was wide open, if Omar had said charge we would have busted through the walls! We was ready to truly take over Saints Grove, not just live there.

I looked at Chelsea looking just as I had done when we were in the puppy love era. Omar's words rocked our relationship and we knew we had to start making changes. The adrenalin finally simmered down as Omar dismissed us for the night but not before giving us our next task, "I want you all to bring at least 2 more people tomorrow for tomorrow's meeting." We all nodded our heads in obedience all thinking how more people could fit in this small house. Never the least we would all obey his wishes.

I escorted Chelsea to the line to meet Omar. It was funny seeing Roman in front of us introducing his lady to Omar. 24

hours ago he would have had nothing positive to say to this man but now he wanted to introduce everybody to his new found idol. Our turn finally came and Omar said "Nice to meet you Chelsea, I see your having a boy!" Chelsea and I both looked wide eyed amazed by his supernatural ability.

"Yes it is a boy and nice to meet you too, how did you know what we were having?" She asked in amazement.

"50/50 I just got lucky" he modestly explained.

My mind started to think insane thoughts of who this man truly was, his quote and assignment related to my whole day entirely to the very dream I had that morning. Never a superstitious man I brushed it off as a weird sequence of events.

"May I please borrow your husband for just a few moments, I promise I won't keep him long." Omar requested. Chelsea granted his wish and went over to the other end of the room with the Muslim lady.

"So what did you produced." He questioned

I gave him my note pad and he flipped through all 20 pages of writing. "Very good he exclaimed, I especially like the comparison to the wolves."

"Thank you" I said

"Okay your next topic I need you to complete for tomorrow on how we spend money. *African Americans understand that a baby cow can't give milk, and that a seed planted can't grow fruit tomorrow, but expect their investment to grow tomorrow.*"

My confusion must had been his cue to leave because he disappeared into the next room.

On the way home my wife and I recapped the whole night talking about our favorite parts. We changed subjects debating about who our group of people were going to be.

"Jeff and his friends he hangs out with, they are all getting together to play spades tomorrow. When you get off work we will go over there and bring them to the meeting tomorrow." I suggested.

"Babe you know your brother will not want any part of that, how will you get him to come." She asked.

"I know how" I simply answered.

We arrived home and dove right into bed. My mind was still amped from Omar's words. My new assignment went through my head thinking about what his quote meant. I went over the quote over and over until a random thought crept into my head. How did Omar know about the wolves I had wrote about. He had literally flipped through 20 pages of my chicken scratch in 10 seconds. I had started writing 2 pages before my writing about the wolf comparison when I realized that I had ran into my earlier writing. I flipped through the end of my last section and began writing the rest of Omar's words. That passage he had recognized was right in the middle. I failed to put any spaces between the two sections so it read continuously. So, with all those factors in place the writing was a too messy for him too have picked out passages fanning through the pages. My curiosity wondered into my dreams as my body shut down.

Chapter 13

Roman

Drops of water beat on my wind shield as the wipers fight to disperse the gathering of puddles from the tears of the night. Surfing waves form when I pull up to the curve all over the side walk. I realize how loud my heat is when I turn down the intensity to cool off the temperature inside. The silence makes my thoughts louder and clearer than ever as I look across the street at Roger. I park next to Harry's, one of the only black owned joints beside Taylors Soul in the neighborhood; I remember getting cut up here all the time as a kid. He caught wind of how me and my friends where paying for our haircuts and refused to serve us until we could prove different employment to him. In retaliation I remember me and Tone sprayed up the whole side of his building with our sign. It was then we saw roger taking out the trash and he saw us spraying up the shop. That was years ago and now he was one our most loyal street soldiers. I know it sickened Harry for Roger to be out here in these streets.

Roger was one of our best dealers; he couldn't keep product on him long enough before his clients emptied his inventory and filled his pockets with cash. Due to his profit margin he was favored by Tone, which led to All-star treatment. But the block was a war zone these days and no one was safe. Bones death weighed heavy on my heart because I knew he wasn't truly about this life. His mechanical gifts gave him a chance out but Tones politician like speeches convince many to follow his guidance. Tones guidance couldn't keep his soldiers safe anymore, his reputation didn't deter violence but invited. If we were affiliated with the empire then we were Bulls eyes and with the cops putting us under a microscope there was very little Tone could do as far as retaliation without it drawing more attention to himself.

I thought a lot about that night we road, it wasn't supposed to be like this. My bullets weren't supposed to find her body. The reason why bone died is the ripple effect to my trigger finger making me the ultimate killer. I feel responsible for Roger because unlike bone who had sought this life out I was the one that brought the streets to Roger and it was my responsibility to get him out before his last breath was taken for my errors.

The cold air mixed with freezing water stung my face as I came in contact with the weather when I got out the car. The cold made me shove my hands deep in my pockets, Shoulders rise to conceal my neck, and head bury low to clothe my chin mouth and cheeks. Roger sees me as I approach him in front of the Indian owned corner store.

"Whats up nigga, what you runnin up like that on me in all black and shit lookin suspect?"

"Man trying to stay warm in this messed up Washington weather, whats up with you bruh?"

"Shit just copping this lotto ticket, Im good in all on money but shit if I hit this muthafucka im so out!" He said laughing.

"Shit I wouldn't blame you, can I holla at you for a minute?"

"Damn you came out here to holla at me, I need to holla at you. I heard what happened to your crib, them punk ass niggas blastin at your fam. How you holdin up?"

"Not good bruh, my ol lady is still shook and my daughter shit don't even get me started."

"Yeah man and with Bone getting clapped too the other day, this shit is getting to real. I been trying to link up with Tone to see what he tryna do."

"Its just that Rog, I think you should chill out. Cats know you out here which makes you a target. Shit it was easy to find you here so what you think gonna happen when they put you on the hit list."

"What, nigga you gave me all the 411 on the game when you put me on. Im ready for that fam."

"Man I gave you guidance to an early grave or a metal box. There is plenty of street soldiers that gave they life to the streets but there is no wall of honor for them. They face get printed on a few T shirts and then your name gets forgotten. Your fam don't get no check from a policy or pension just the pain of living on without you. Look love one you haven't been caught up in the system, you still got a fighting chance to turn your shit around."

"what? Nigga you said this life don't have no retirement plan. What you talkin about I can just dip out?"

I grab the fabric from his collar and ram his back to the brick wall. "And now im giving you that retirement plan. Stay of the block Rog, I got lucky when my house got hit! My fuckin Daughter could had got one to the chest! You think this shit a game! My daughter! Rog don't be out her again homie or on my strips Im going to take you out my damn self!"

Roger

The night seemed icier with my senses zeroing in on the bitter cold of the wind. The graffiti I had once admired on the side of the wall of a building adjacent to me all of a sudden seemed repulsive. Something was different in his eyes, it wasn't the fact that they were misty and stressed but the fact that it was my first time seeing them like that. His voice carried weight with the promise to drop it on my shoulders if I didn't comply. The person who brought me into the game was not the person standing in front of me, this person resembled someone who had faced death and came back with a message. I had a little boy myself and images of him on the floor bleeding flashed through my mind. His grip loosened on my shirt freeing me from his rage.

"Alright fam, I heard you speak. I still got a lil product on me so ima give it to Tone."

"No you not, give it to me, your next step is going in the direction of your home. Your trail better not lead you back here."

With that Rome relived me of my product and pulled off into the night. The sudden career change had me frozen in place. Even though I don't know where my next dollar is going to come from I feel relived, for the first time in a long while I didn't care if a cop stopped and frisked me. I wasn't flashy like some members in the set; so I had a little nest egg to hold me over for a minute. I had always wanted to cut hair and own my own shop, my skills were legendary, my uncle had still owned the barbershop and he had always wanted me to follow in his footsteps. I look back over at the building and thought tomorrow I'm going to paint over the graffiti. My uncle had been meaning to do that to his shop for a while.

Chapter 14

Stone

The time for me to wake up to start a new day came too soon. The late hours the previous night turned into the early morning before I finally decided to shut my eyes, or blink by the way I felt. The shower did its job in stimulating my body to shake the fatigue off. I throw my usual dress attire on and escaped to my car on the road. The coffee was extremely bitter this morning, it felt as though I was drinking water with dirt in it as I felt the coffee grains swish around in my mouth. The red light catches me as I stop just short of rear ending the car in front of me. I take the stop to catch my breath and I look in the mirror at the zombie looking back. The sleep deprivation took life from my eyes, created bags around them that not even this bitter coffee could get rid of.

The rest of the work day drained the empty energy I had to start with. It seemed as though Andre was taunting me. The evidence I had on him was circumstantial and speculation at best and wasn't enough to prosecute. Bone was dead and the department's fire on these shooting cases had burned through its wax and was barely flickering. There was so many drug dealers and drug users being brought in that the homicides were being grouped in with drug enforcement, as I kept being assigned new cases on my desk. With the amount of paper work on the people of SG I felt justified in just cordoning the whole town off and having everybody incarcerated. I mean am I trying to fill in a bottomless pit? Crime can't even stay relevant in this community long enough to be solved because more crime is committed taking the attention off of the previous incident.

"Man, you look like shit partner." Cordell acknowledge slamming a file on my overcrowded desk.

"And you look to refreshed, you must not be doing any work. It's a surprise anybody in this department gets any sleep with the amount of people we drag back and forth from here."

"That's because I don't take this shit home with me like you and some of the others do." Cordell bragged.

"Well I think I got a person of interest on this young lady case."

"Stone, come on, we should focus on the other cases we got that are actually solvable, besides nobody is breathing down our asses anymore."

"It was a little girl Cordell, and it is solvable. You remember that drive by shooting that shot up a Roman Walkers house?"

"Yea."

"Well come to find out Roman is 2 Tone's right hand man. I mean think about it, Roman house gets shot up, and then Bone dies all in close proximity to the West Tacoma shooting. All these events are related I know they are."

"If we think hard enough we can make anything relate. If you wanna keep doing this soon to be cold case than that's on you partner. All those people know each other, they are all family, ex's, my mommas cousins friend I mean they are all connected in one way or another. I'm focusing on the other mountain of paper work on my desk."

"Nice to see your so into letting murders go free."

"No I'm in to clearing out my desk. Shit If I'm speaking from my heart the SG is a jungle and in the jungle there is no law eventually ending in everybody getting what they deserve. I mean who are we foolin, they don't live by no code and we do our job to get a pay check Stone. All that academy BS they teach you, we keep them in line so that the rest of hard working America can prosper."

"And how are we keeping them in line when killings are allowed to come with no justice to follow!?"

"Stone look around you! Believe it or not this is there prison! The best part about this prison is that they pay to stay there instead of going to jail to waste tax payer's money!"

"Well I tell you what I get paid because I'm a police officer and the drug dealers and gang members get paid by the streets but people like you are the worst because they get paid from both sides!"

Cordell movements became cemented like a statue. His eyes pierced through my eyes to see into my brain as to what I was thinking. As a detective you come to find out that evidence, witnesses, and words don't always get you caught up like a facial expression does. His posture had deceit, eyes hid secrets and tone of voice yielded uncertainty.

"Where are you getting at?"

"Why did Bone call you Ross Cordell?"

"So here we are. You ran out of leads, so you're firing in the darkness. Your basing suspicion off what a crazy gang banger says."

"No I'm just asking a question to which your words won't answer honestly." I said as I pushed away from my desk and walked out of the precinct.

2 Tone

I feel the rough terrain as I glide my tongue over my teeth; the taste of Newport flavors my salvia as I gulp it down in the place of food. My stomach controls my thoughts as I smell the KFC fried chicken when I pull the door open. I purchase a family bowl all to myself and feast in my Monte Carlo. Though my hunger has ceased I keep looking across the street at Taylor's Soul. I remember going there when I was younger to indulge in his famous fried chicken, hands down the best thing you could treat your taste buds to. That was a long time ago, Mr. Taylor took a holier than thou approach and said he couldn't accept my tainted money at his establishment. I look at his place shaking my head thinking who in the hell he thought he was. His shop had been struggling for years and he turning down money, I see KFC didn't care what dollar I paid with. In my opinion all money was tainted money at one point so there is no reason to deny funds.

I look next door to his restaurant and see the church all freshly painted with manicured bushes and trees. The church seems so out of place in this neighborhood like a pastor would be in the club. The houses fencing the church for blocks look like a pile of wood with the Church being the diamond. They is all hypocrites soaking up the so called lords money from these people living check to check mean while the preachers stand is made of stained oak wood. Church has always been the backwards Robin Hood taking money for the poor and dumping it into their castle. I had never seen the Pastor look dingy but I always seen the members in their rags throughout the week. What is that nigga job anyway, to sit there all week judging folks then pulling everyone in on Sunday to say how they living then collecting money from that. Shit I just can't understand how these God fearing folk see me as a hustle and not the person playing off the emotions. Like God need plush seats, red velvet carpet with his servant dress to the nines. Shit the church is supposed to serve the block but instead we just serve them our 10 percent. Cats put money in the church every Sunday but can't go withdraw nothing when they electric bill is overdue. God will provide the Pastor preaches when he know damn well it don't work like that, he tell his members to provide in tidying and then turn around and tell them that God will provide for their needs.

The car rumbles my body as I turn the keys in my ignition and pull out. I had been up the past 23 hours moving product around a collecting rent from my block holders. My phone illuminates my interior as I open my phone to call Roman. The Ringing consumes the whole call before it sends me to voicemail. Where the hell is this nigga I think? I scroll through my contacts again and land on LaShandria's number. I smile thinking about what she would feel and think when she sees my number flash on her screen. I press the green phone icon and the ringing begins, the ringing goes on up until I expect the voicemail to pick up but instead her soft voice answers the phone with hello. Lust rushes over my body as I begin talking to her.

"Whats up what you doin"

She responds with hesitation just how she did when I had first solicited her response on that couch. She becomes blunt and short cutting her thoughts in half with short phrases.

"Look I just want to know where Roman is why you thinking I'm calling for your ass." I shot back.

She denies his availability and his where a bouts to me when I know damn well he probably in the other room. Something is defiantly different from our last interaction, I know it's the after regrets, she wants to rid herself of her mistake but I'm not some cold you can just catch right quick then quickly squash.

"So it's like that huh?"

Lashandria

"Yes" I respond hating myself more and more the longer I'm on the line with him. Omar's words shame my existence whether that was his intentions or not. I had fallen from the top of the apple tree to where this rodent now had taken a bite out of me. I know I tasted good to him and I must admit it satisfied me to see him indulge in me. I had known the moment I seen his name pop up on my phone what he wanted. Roman was not his priority as a matter a fact Roman was in the way of his desires. The more Tone disgusted me with his betrayal to his best friend the more I sickened myself with my own actions.

Roman was in the next room and I started to sharpen my tongue towards him and giving him my irritated tone. The message was eventually received and he hung up. I sat with my phone to my ear hearing nothing for a moment as I tried to fight back the flood that was swelling up in my eyes. I need to tell Roman the truth but I rather be a slave to this lie than free without Roman. There is no way he would look past my actions to my heart where I had so much love for him.

The door knob twist and Roman enters, his freshly edged facial hair cloaked over his milk chocolate skin accompanied with his smooth bald head made me desire him. I forced myself on him ripping my own clothes off and shove my tongue deep in his mouth. I have to love him better than I did Tone and he has to satisfy me better than Tone did. In a sickening way being in the same bed that I did another makes me even wetter, I fill my mouth with his man hood, my tongue dancing along his long vein. I form my jaws to him doing every technique I can think off to drive him to the edge of climax. I feel him pulsate alarming me of his arrival, I stop just short and blow warm breath on his head to calm him down.

Roman

"Why you stop babe!" She places her tongue on my head and licks from my shaft all the way up to my neck. Her lips begin extracting the skin from my neck consuming it whole making a neck birth mark inevitable. Her warm hands place me deep inside, it felt like I splashed in a warm bath as wet as she was slipping in and out. I'm feeling myself lose control, I'm trying to hold on for dear life but she is riding me to good!

Lashandria

I bounce up and down losing control over my body as I start shaking, I can feel him about to cum and I can't help myself but come along with him as I moan Tones name the same time he moans for his climax. My blood immediately turns cold knocking me out of me heat felt passion. I start kissing him saying that he turns me on trying to make turn sound like Tone so that I can argue that he miss heard me if he noticed my outburst.

Roman

She kisses me all over my face moaning how I turn her on but I could have sworn I heard her say Tone. My blood heats up with anger but her tender kisses keep cooling me down. She kisses me passionately something she hadn't done really since I got out of prison. I was so happy to feel her desire for me once again that I begin to convince myself of how I always be miss hearing things. I embrace her naked body in my arms for the rest of the night.

Lashandra

I feel so secure in his arms and yet insecure in my own skin. How did I lose control and say his fuckin name! Oh my god my mission was to rid myself of him and I ended up fantasizing about him. His warm body reassures me that he didn't realize what I had said. This secret has to be buried, Omar's words couldn't have come at a more messed up time. He was so moving and so empowering that had I heard him before I saw Tone I know I never would had lowered to this level. I kiss his arms that are fixed to my body holding me in place and rest my eyes.

I don't remember even falling asleep but know that I was because the time said two in the morning. The pain wakes me and it is excruciating causing me to toss and turn. The agony is making me kick off the blanket so that my sweat can cool to the cold air of the window. I have always had bad cramps but this can't be possible, because my period can't be here. I confirmed three times and I'm positive. Shit did I eat something, is it a muscle spasm? These are the suggestions I throw to myself to avoid other possibilities. Damn now I'm cold again pulling the blanket over my body.

"Babe are you okay?" Roman says to me felling my movement waking him from his sleep.

"Yea its probably food poisoning or something"

"Nobody else had food poisoning."

"Well maybe it doesn't agree with me!" I snapped.

"Babe I think we need to go to the hospital."

"I think you need to go back to sleep, I'm not trying to go through all that."

Like I needed to hear what the hell they had to say. You think I needed to be triaged and placed on hold until someone gets to me about my lost. Telling me they are so sorry and guiding me out the damn door then billing me 2000 dollars for that. I don't have any damn insurance for that. I know I'm being punish but what the hell did my baby have to do with anything! The stress of the shooting, me allowing Tone to taint me weighed so heavy on my conscience that my body had to relieve some weight so I can stay afloat. I know he is looking at my tears stream down my cheeks.

"Baby, it will be okay baby." He says trying to comfort me.

He knows that it's not my physical pain that has these tears rolling, as he's telling me this it's going to be okay fairy tale. I can feel wetness flow down to the crack of my butt. I leap from the bed and sprint to the bathroom locking it behind me.

Roman

I race after her but she was quicker than I was getting up allowing her to lock me out. I look back on the bed and remove the covers where she was laying to find blood on the ivory sheets. I knock on the door telling her to let me in. The absents of sound turn my knocks into banging shouting commands at her to open the door. I use my foot as a key and kick the door open. She is in the tube with blood.

"Im sorry baby. Im so sorry! I couldn't hold on to the baby!" she cries

She is drenched in sweat, tears and her shorts in blood. All this damn stress I've been putting on her that my seed had to bare! My lifes fuck ups have been the debt paid for by a person who never experienced life! All my hood cred, my aggressiveness, my ability to hustle the streets for money is worthless to my woman now. I can't do nothing for her but watch as she suffers blaming herself.

"Baby its me bae, you didn't do anything, Im so sorry!"

"No, it's my duty to carry our child and I dropped it."

I can't even take the damn blame form her, I can't take the pain from her, it seems I can only take her dreams, her chances, her forgiveness and her life. I remember her holding her stomach the day I rushed home when they shot up my house, I knew the gun shots made her jump to the ground causing trauma to my unborn. My baby had been dying for days while I was out running with fuckin Tone! It's crazy how this life can claim a life that hadn't even lived yet.

Chapter 15

Darrius

I created a trail as my foot submerged into the clouds that covered the ground inhaling the wintry air and exhaling warm Fog. Back home the dreaded snow meant the cancelation of school, closure of roads, increased traffic with a higher than normal chance of a vehicle accidents; but here in Aspen the white foam was the main tourist attraction where adults were encouraged to slide down the mountain snowboarding or skiing. Lifts that rose all the way to the heavens gave a spectacular view of nature powdered in winter's gift. Santa clause version of a beach I thought were the ground seeming to be made of cotton met the frozen floor allowing any man to walk on water. Jeff and his best friends Tyson and Roger joined Chelsea and I as we welcomed the cold in our Canadian goose coats speeding down the slopes. The Cabin like hotel we stayed in were resorts in its self-containing spas, 5 star restaurants, in room jacuzzies, Bars full of the liquid sin, and night life clubs. I loved it out here!

Jeff, Tyson and Roger were amateurs in indulging in these paradises; paying top dollar for extravagant services and activities. This was an ironic turn of events thinking back in the past. In their beginnings in Saints Grove these dogs were always sniffing for the best deal, never paying more than what they had to. They were masters at negotiating prices driving the prices down and the volume of merchandise up. The issue was that this parleying only took place with the black people they knew. "Let me get your discount or hook me up," they would say if they saw one of their friends at the counter. Or "come on Mr. Taylor you have known my peoples for years you know I got you next time," they would promise Mr. Taylor the owner of a soul food restaurant in Saints Grove. Never did they bargain with Wal-Mart, McDonalds or other tycoon corporations, they only did it with their people.

Thinking back to Jeff, Tyson and Roger's past the Aspen environment suddenly felt cold. I look around me and notice we were the only ink spots here. Many of these white people have had family property at this location for years so their vacation is merely just coming home and doing what they have always done. My group were here for a different reason, we dreaded home and thus is the reason why we escaped here. For the first time I realized I was dreaming, I knew this wasn't real. I dropped down to my knees and brought both my hands down breaking through the snow! My blow shock the whole mountain crumbling the mountains and uprooting the trees! I shot out of my sleep in a cold sweat panting hard like a dog down south in the middle of August.

I started my morning on the phone talking to a ghost it seemed. Fred had called randomly and we flew down memory lane. Back in the day one couldn't have been too far from the other. At the same time we couldn't have been more different. Fred was a proud member of the Bloods from California and I was just a person who didn't really fit into any category other than just being black from Washington. I weighed my options in a tense situation during a fight, seeing how big my opponent is, are the cops around, how many people does he have backing him compared to my crew. Fred was spontaneous thinking, he struct first and thought about the options as they came while dealing with the consequences that arouse. The words I use to describe him would have you believe he was a giant man with Hercules strength and Spartan like fighting styles but he had to be 130 soaking wet. However, he would be the last person I would want to fight because of his spirit. You would have to kill him before he admitted defeat.

Fred pledge allegiance to the red flag before the red white and blue. The oath to the gang took precedence over the constitution and street life took priority over the law. Fred lived his life according to the rhythm of the streets instead of the flow of society. Fred would take many oaths in his life, an oath to the Bloods, Oath to marriage, Oath to becoming a father and an Oath to defend this nation from all enemies foreign and domestic.

I met Fred in a place where you would think would be the last place he would be; at the Security Forces Squadron, when I was stationed at Barksdale Air Force Base. Fred did his job as he saw fit, listen to the orders that he agreed with and disregarded others. The only reason he would abide by a set rule would only be if it shared common ground with his wants. He was admired by myself and others who hung around him for his fearlessness, courage, and ability to stand his ground, simultaneously he was labeled a horrible sentry for his continuing disregard of protocol, regulations and noncompliant to the personnel assigned as his superior. The superiors did what they did best with people who didn't submit to their orders and discharged him early out of the military.

Fred resembled many before him and one by one the chain of command discharged others who shared his complexion. Blacks where the minority most of the time being only five or six on a flight of 30. We tend to stick together most of time standing out even more in the eyes of the squadron. A few black dots go unnoticed but when a group of them get together they are notice as a stain. The higher ups where not like the ancestors before them. They didn't shout nigger, lynch or openly display their hatred. They did it more undercover. They displayed prejudice by amplifying the black troops mistakes and ignoring the sea of white troops who were also doing wrong. The punishment of a dark complexion troop would be publicly displayed to send a message. The worst part was using our own to do the punishment. They would many times reward a small portion of us to keep the others in line. In my case, it was First Sergeant Tracy Owens. She acted as a prosecutor more than she did an airmen liaison which was her primary function. She would be harsher than the white superiors in punishment, Owens took the short comings of black performance personal and thus showed no mercy in punishing the black individuals that came into her office.

One after one black troops went into her office to find their careers destroyed when they came out. She found no fault in her Air Force only in her black people who served in it that was standing in her office. A helping hand from one of our own that made it would turn to a boot slamming on your fingers while you are barely trying to hold on. She received countless awards from her superiors because she kicked out people like Fred and had a prosperous career. She proudly boosted that she had gotten many airmen kicked out. Cleaning out the Air Force she would say much like society had been doing with blacks since the beginning. I was one of the few that made it out of that squadron with all my rank and benefits. Many of my brothers and sisters fell victim to Sergeant Owens penalties.

Fred, his community, and others like him always baffled me. The people running the hood as it is so popular titled always displayed CEO type ambition, loyal workers, and respect among their entire community. A tool can always be used for negative results as CEO's where drug lords, the loyal workers were dealers and gang members and the respect factor was actually fear.

I would always imagine that the drug lord was a business owner, and that the other competing business owners owned different business in the same community, then the dealers or gangsters were instead workers of these businesses who would then spend their earning at the other black own businesses. The businesses would gain wealth and pay their workers well so that the workers could start to own their houses in that community. A dream I have without even being a sleep or dazing off. A black community owning their own homes, businesses, developing their assets, then turn around and reinvest that money into other businesses in their community and spending their free dollar at other black businesses! Well that sounds like the first Black Wall street and we all know how that turned out. The hood has always been literal to me. The hood hides the beauty of the black community. If we were to take that hood off, we would see beauty beyond recognition with an infinite amount of possibilities.

Me and Fred spoke for a while reminiscing of old times and things we wish we would have done different. I tried to advise Fred who was now driving for a living about starting his own driving company. He shot back with he was just trying to find a decent employer and that he didn't want the head ache. Omar's words ran through my head about the black man not desiring more. Fred found a way to get off the phone with me saying work was stealing his attention. His environment always seemed to find a way to snatch him off the phone the moment a conversation about thinking beyond the box came into play.

4 o clock came creeping by when I realized I hadn't yet asked Jeff and his friends to join my wife and I at church. I dialed Jeff's number and it took me straight to voicemail. Jeff was like this. Whenever he needed something he would light your phone up leaving countless text messages and voicemails and the moment you called him back he would pickup first ring. When Jeff was stable, with money in his pocket he would be almost impossible to get a hold of on the phone. knowing this pattern I was already in route to his apartment.

I pulled up to the rundown apartment complex and could hear the bass coming from his unit. Neighbors here never called the cops for loud noise complaints. To them loud music was as natural as birds chirping. I knocked at the door and even though from any part of the house it took only a few steps to get to the door they were very slow at opening it. The door swung open and I was greeted by Tyson.

"Whats good my G!"

"What up T how you been," I responded.

"Shit you know me I stays grindin."

I walked into the apartment and saw Jeff and Roger on the PS4. This scene could not have looked more counterproductive. Three men cramped on the sofa, blowing smog forming a white haze inside the whole place. Their faces were mellow and eyes dyed pink. At these moments with all their different problems none mattered. Their vapor cured their worry, block their determination, depleted there energy and gave them a relaxation better than any vacation. I knew if I was to get them to come with me I would have to trick them.

Years ago I would confide in Jeff about my promiscuous ways when I was in the military, Jeff would many times boost to his friends how his older brother was slaying women left and right. He idolized me when I relayed to him that I was seeing many women at once while I was married to Chelsea. Jeff like I was, were addicts when it came to women. We couldn't just have one we had to taste, feel, devour, and penetrate as many as we could. I would spoon feed lies to the other women to get them to come and I would inject lies into Chelsea to make her stay. It took me almost losing Chelsea to divorce before I had finally sought counseling to cure my addiction. I made my silent vow that I would never be unfaithful again. With this being my current legacy I used it to my advantage.

"Aye one of my home girls say she havin a lil get together with her girlfriends and was wonderin if I could slide through." I seduced.

"Okay I see you, you need to put the team on Darrius, you can't knock them all down." Said Tyson.

"I know this that's why I need my young bloods to roll wit me."

"Shit! You know we finna ride out wit you, and nigga these hoes better be bad to." Roger announced.

"Bruh, you know Darrius only messes wit dem dimes." Jeff defended.

If Omar wanted to have a great example of what many of our men in our community think of the ladies he couldn't have found a better one then right here in this apartment. I couldn't get them to come if I said this man Omar is going to preach about black prosperity, black unity, respecting women, and black education, but ladies half naked shaking they asses would draw their attendance.

"Aye Darrius you been talkin to that nigga Roman?' Roger asked.

"Yea a lil bit, why you ask."

Roger looked at Tyson and the both in harmony said "Niiigggggaaaaaa!"

Tyson went on to say. "This nigga going around preachin talkin bout wat we doing is hinder black progress and how we need to stop selling our shit."

"Nigga I was even more surprised because we got the shit from Roman." Roger said laughing.

"What did yall say?" I asked.

"Man to be honest I just chucked it up to he smoke some good ass shit that made him forget who he was. But I know about that shit that happen to him so I can understand but a complete 360 I never saw that comin. He rides up on me on the block hems me up against the wall and basically fires me from the game." Roger replied.

"Shit I need to smoke me some of that to!" Tyson followed up smiling.

"Yea that nigga be trippin sometimes, but he definitely on some different shit wit all that preachin, him and 2 Tone the one that have the most impact over this shit anyway. Shit that's probably why he hasn't been returning my calls, I've been trying to re up, I had to go across town to get this weak shit." Jeff explained.

"Anyways when this function suppose to go down my G." Tyson asked.

"in 2 hours."

"Shit lets ride out to get some to eat." Jeff suggested.

We all piled into Jeffs upscale vehicle. The stereo and engine started at the same time blaring the bass all over the streets. We drove right up the street and pulled into the KFC parking lot. We stepped out the car and began walking to the doors before I stopped.

"Yo, if we tryna eat chicken we know who go the best strips in the SD, Mr, Taylors joint is just right up the street. " I said

"Nigga Mr. Taylor a few bucks out of my range and besides I got a home girl that work here that always hook a nigga up, shit all you got to do is give her some dro." Jeff boosted proudly.

"Bro come on Mr. Taylor is just a few bucks more, we get way better quality and quantity and his restaurant is home grown from our community. He about the only black business owner here, we need to support." I preached.

They all laughed "Nigga now you sounding like Roman" Tyson said as they continued into KFC.

It was never enough for Mr. Taylor to have the best quality of product in his town. It was never enough for him to stay loyal to his community never moving his establishment despite constant attempts his daughter had at trying to expand or relocate. Her name was Tamie and she was just a few years older than me. We had gone to the same church growing up, her and her father always catered the church events. Everybody loved eating at Taylor's Soul the restaurant was called. At one time Mr. Taylor was the only black owned business and chicken spot. Tamie Idolized her father and couldn't wait to take over the family business. All that would be halted once the KFC bought the old abandon auto shop a few buildings down. Taylor's Soul was snatched away as the community ran to the cheap, steroid injected establishment.

Tamie and her father were always at odds with the direction of the business. Tamie had lost faith in her people seeing them as traitors that turned their support away from an establishment that was loyal to them. Taylor still had confidence in Saints Grove, seeing his business decline as a test of endurance from God. Mr. Taylor refused to relocate saying Saints Grove was his area where he would serve. Tamie was consistently proven right as day after day she saw some of Mr. Taylors most loyal customers open the doors of KFC. Even in spite of this Mr. Taylor started firing up the Ovens and turning every stove eye red creating his legendary dishes.

I opened the doors of Taylor's Soul and the aroma of fried chicken filled the air. Smokey Robinson cruisin was playing over the intercom. There was a few older gentleman at the counter each indulging in their pates.

"Welcome to Taylor's Soul" Tamie said with her head down looking to pull a menu out.

"Hey Tamie I see you running this place now!" I exclaimed.

Her eyes looked up and locked with mine. "Darrius!!!! Oh my God how have you been!" she said embracing me in her arms. I hadn't seen her since I had left for the military 6 years ago were I ate my final SG meal before I departed that next morning.

"Ive been good, how about you?"

"Well you know just trying to hold on to my father's dream and build this place up with this back turning community." She said smirking.

"We just have to find our way back, I'm sure business will kick up."

"Shoot the last time this place was packed was probably your going away party all those years ago, ever since then attendance here has been declining. Only my dads old friends come in and dine. Most of the time dad doesn't even charge. It seems that a few dollars is all it takes to keep people here. We can't afford to keep doing this for much longer though. I fear we may have to sell this place, we only live off our pass success when we were booming, thank God my dad had the sense to save most and invest the rest giving us a nest egg. But over the years it has depleted my families wealth. You know my dad though, always seeing Saints Grove as his home."

"And how do you see it." I asked.

"Shoot I see us a guest that have over stayed their welcome." She said with a forced smile. I looked at my watch and saw that we only had 20 mins to get to church.

"I tell you what, how late will you be here." I asked.

"We usually don't close shop until 10:30 or so." She answered.

"Okay my wife and I will be back we have to attend this meeting." I promised

"Okay it was good seeing you Darrius and I'm sure dad wants to lay eyes on you as well."

I gave her a parting hug and took off down the street to my brother and his friends. When I arrived at his car I was disgusted with the view of them. How could they totally take away their support. Every single one of them purchased the products at full retail price from the white man corporationsq. We denied our own neighbors in our community and accepted the businesses that didn't even know our names. We were merely numbers in a chart to them. I saw the restaurant across the street almost empty. I had just happened to look down the street back at Mr. Taylors spot and could see the side door opened as I saw Mrs. Taylor dump loads of food out. Money and sacrifice being thrown away trying to build something with in the community. Why did we do this? The crew I had rolled with expected a premium product at a cheap price because the owner looked like us. The community suffocated any business established by one of our own.

I thought back to my mother staying up late nights trying to create her cakes. Many people in our neighborhood placed orders but never came through with the payment. I remember her on the phone saying "But I already made the cake the way you wanted!" They would reply I'm sorry Teresa we found a better deal at Walmart, or Safeway. My mother grew bitter of her own people constantly selling her dreams of winning their business. She would say "white people know how to keep their word; black people know how to disappoint!" History had made us slaves, unequal citizens, and burdens of the whites but now they are our biggest savior as far as business associates. The banks give us money when we need a loan, while our neighbors shut down to any sign of investing with one another. The white costumers pay in advance while the blacks pay late. The whites say what a good deal while the blacks say the deal is not good enough. The look on my mother's face of disappointment after she would get off the phone was that of a beaten warrior. Her face would turn to my brothers and

I and she would say "There's cake in the kitchen!" The warm moist cake melted in your mouth. The ingredients formed a bond with my taste buds dreading the time when you had that last bite. How could they not see that the cake was worth way more than the price?

I to became a sheep following the crowd to these crowded institutions selling chemical induced food products in bulk. I had been home for about 8 months and I myself hadn't paid Mr. Taylor a visit. I stopped at plenty of McDonalds, Jack in the Box, and Wendy's though. I drove right through my community businesses to the giant owners. I saw graffiti defacing local business buildings while the Target was shining with freshly coated paint. I saw us litter at our own establishments but throw our trash in a bin at the mall.

I pulled out my note pad and began pouring out my thoughts. *"When it comes to business ownership our community is the forgotten garden filled with weeds and insects. We fail to water our own establishments, we fail to shine on our own products and services and most of all we fail to even plant any assets. But some people like Mr. Taylor plant a seed, water, shine and nurture a garden to the point to which it bares fruit. Sweet juicy succulent fruit, and our community fails to consume it. The weeds in our garden have grown so high that it covers the fruit and hides the fertile soil ground beneath it giving the area the appearance of a land that isn't producing. I feel that our people's attitudes have grown so ignorant that they shun any fruit being produce and simply walk over the fertile soil. We water other companies with our finances quenching their thirst of money and we shine our attentions on businesses* that only flourish in the dark. We don't plant our seeds we only treat them like sun flower seeds getting a quick taste and spitting out the rest. I fear that my community will never see our land as opportunity but a place of ruin."

I snapped out of my thoughts, stuffed my note pad in my pocket and we all piled in my brothers car. As we drove my mind was racing with what to say to my passengers in the car when they realized it wasn't any sort of party.

"Damn the block is flooded, aint no where to park." Roger announced

"Shit Darrius you was right this party is jumpin off and it aint even 8 o clock yet" Tyson joined in.

I looked around and couldn't understand why Omar would invite this many people to his house. It could barely hold the few of us the last meeting. I was also amazed at the turnout. I wondered what others had to tell there guest to get them to come.

"Man we just gonna park down the street and walk up. I aint tryna get traffic jammed up if niggas start lighting up the spot you feel me" Jeff said

"I second that my nigga" Tyson supported.

We parked a few blocks down the street from Omars house and began journeying to his residence.

"You know for it to be such a lit party wit hella people I sho don't hear no music." Tyson reported.

"Nigga you got a point. They probably already got a loud noise complaint from the boys" Jeff responded.

I still was trying to find the words to explain the event we were truly going to. When they find out the true nature of this gathering they may turn right back around. As we kept walking the street ended with a sea of people in the road and sidewalks in front of Omar's house.

"Nigga what the hell is this" Roger questioned.

"Look yall ima be real, this is a lecture from this guy that I really feel you should hear" I explained.

"This Nigga reeled us! Nigga you wasn't tryna be real when you sold us this dream and shit of a party!" Jeff shot back.

"Look homie you my nigga and all but I aint finna listen to no school lecture or church sermon in the middle of the damn street. Yo boi Roman already hit me wit one of them." Roger joined in.

As Jeff, Tyson and Roger started to retreat to their car Omar came out unto his porch with a thunderous voice, Wake UP!!!!

Chapter 16

Omar

"WAKE UP PRODUCER AND CONSUMER and the three-gentleman walking away in the back!!"

Omar jumped down from his porch and walked through the crowd to where we were standing.

Jeff, Tyson and Roger please step up here with me I need to ask you something Omar said

"Man what the hell is this Darrius? I aint tryna volunteer for nothin." Roger whispered to me.

It will just be a second and once we are done you can be on your way if you wish. Omar insisted.

The three of them hesitantly walked up the porch in front of the crowd.

"Tyson please for the audience tell me briefly about your week." Omar asked.

Tyson looked oddly at Omar

"Well shit I just go to work for 40 hours a week and try to snatch up any overtime, catch the bus, put my kids to bed go to sleep and wait until the weekend."

"Wow well I don't know if you know this or not but Christopher Benson went on a 2 week vacation in the beginning of this month and is now taking off again for another week tomorrow for his daughters 16th birthday." Omar announced.

Tyson looked at Omar and said "What does that got to do wit me or the question you just asked."

"Everything!" Omar shouted to the crowd.

"Now Tyson when do you plan on going on a two week vacation?'

"Man cats don't get paid like that." Tyson shouted.

"Wrong! They do get paid like that, Chris Benson is the owner of the company you work for. The reason why you won't get to go on vacations and take of when you like is because you labor all your energy and time so Benson can have his American dream. And in return Benson gives you a dollar fifty above minimum wage.

WAKE UP BLACK PEOPLE!!!

Tyson is supposed to repeat this cycle, right? Is Jeff children supposed to accept a part time father with a full-time job? Is Darrius's wife supposed to support his employers corporate goals instead their marriage? Yes, these questions are not written in good taste but the answer is *yes!!!!* Companies have told us yes to those questions and so did we as a people! I told some of my friends and family that I am going to quit my job, check the disenrollment option for school and start a business. I was greeted with a mountain of opposition. How you going to support your family? How you going to gamble with you lively hood like that? Why are you taking this unnecessary risk! Do you know how much running a business cost? How will you get a good education?

I also told these same people when I got out the military that I found a job and am enrolling in school, there replies. That's great, you're going to get great benefits, you can get you a nice apartment with 18 dollars an hour, student debt is worth it if your salary in your career field pays well to afford those payments. Our ambitions have been translated to acceptance of societal norms and we have thus suppressed that entrepreneurial spirit.

The crowd was shaking their heads at the culture Omar was preaching about. Jeff, Tyson and Roger had forgotten all about the made up party and was in a trance as Omar was speaking. Omar continued.

I'm not speaking as a successful man, or as an accomplished entrepreneur, not even as a financially independent man, I'm talking as a man tired of running on a treadmill in a track race. No matter how fast I run I stay in the same place as my hierarchy gets further ahead. I'm speaking as a man who sees his wife and children's pain without being present due to a huge volume of overtime shifts. I'm preaching as a man who places his lively hood in a corporate giant that can't even see me from way up there. I'm crying as a man who just woke up!

The crowd shouts of Amen echoed outside and aroused the neighboring houses attention. The neighbors started to open the door and walk to were all the commotion was.

We have been tricked, hood winked, fooled, lead astray, mislead whatever you want to call it! We thought we had a slice of the American pie until we found out how big the pie is and realized that we are only receiving crumbs. We thought we was free from slavery because of the emancipation proclamation, and the removal of our ancestor's shackles until we realized that we were incarcerated in these systems called corporate employment. As a matter a fact I will go a little deeper…. Please tell me how we are overrepresented in the prison system but almost absent in the business owner category. I will tell you the answer, it's because we settled for obedience instead of dominance. Our dollar skips our mouth and feeds the government, banks, landlords, bill companies, student loans and outside corporations that view your community as a profit margin. Hell, our dollar barely make it to the black owned barbershop or beauty shop before it is intercepted by a Walmart, target, macys, McDonalds etc. The dollar never circulates in black communities. The only income that floods our communities is welfare that we must spend at corporate stores. Employment has created a dependence on a bi weekly paycheck. J.O.B just over Broke! I'm tired! I know your Tired! We as a community need to gather and unit to free ourselves of dependence of corporations and educational facilities that don't have our best interest at heart!!

That's right! Preach! Speak to them pastor!! These phrases poured out of the audiences mouths. I could fill the emotion of the people surrounding me. I looked around and saw old and young, man and woman, and saw that we were all tired. The crowd had grew enormously and was hanging on to every word out of Omars mouth.

"Fellas do you know what supply and demand are?" Omar asked Jeff, Tyson and Roger. in front of everybody.

"I demand something, you supply it for some cash" Jeff answered.

Exactly Jeff but if you will allow me to I am going to further explain this concept. Supply and demand is an economic theory that demonstrates the relationship between resources whether that be services or products and the demand for such resources. This relationship determines the volume of product produced and the pricing of that product to the consumer. This concept governs everything requiring money. Nothing is free in this world and has a cost. This theory is the source of power that propels the free market into effect. Further dissecting this concept the free market is the house where businesses reside to compete to win your dollar. These companies excluding monopolies which are sole runners in a certain market use the supply and demand theory to gain an advantage over one another to win the consumers business. To simplify it further businesses do not want a surplus of inventory or a shortage of resources to the demand, they desire to order just enough supply to satisfy all their demand so that profit is maximized.

The point of this basic economic lesson is to understand how business works and how the African American community fall into just one category of the free market, the consumer. Please noticed that when I asked Mr. Jeff what the definition of supply was he stated that he demands something that others supply for his cash, also notice that even though I said supply and demand he related more to the demand side than the supply. So in other words we are the demand. We demand products and services and feed establish businesses with our hourly wages. This is not a bad thing however, we make the economy grow and flourish with our lavish spending. This is not the problem; the problem exists when we don't make our dollar work for us. We tend not to be the supply which makes the money, only the demand that gives the money.

The simple fact is we work for companies and or government, receive payment from our labor but not before the government takes there share in the form of taxes. The remainder of that money is used to pay off services such as mortgage (banks), utilities, car notes (banks), insurances (private companies) etc. The balance then goes right back to the corporations as we buy our groceries, go to the mall, entertainment etc. Most of the time especially people living pay check to pay check very little if any goes into savings. So, what's left for the community that's starving after all other obese corporations have had their fill? What's left for the famish net worth of black enterprise? The pot is licked clean by external tongues before the internal community even opens their mouths.

I'm going to shoot another definition at you for the word Opportunity cost. This economic term means the potential loss of an option due to choosing another alternative. For example, you use one dollar to buy a soda to drink instead of using that one dollar to buy 4 packets of drink mix to go along with the sugar and water you have at home to create 4 pitchers of juice. So, once a resource is spent on one choice it ignores the other options. How does this all tie together you might ask? How is this supply and demand theory, free market, and opportunity cost supposed to clean up our situation? BY APPLYING IT TO OUR CAUSE!!!

We have all been blind economist for years, we buy in bulk, you go for the lowest price, we compare products to different items to see if we can substitute a product or not. We budget choosing which best way to spend our dollar at the grocery store to maximize the value of each dollar spent which is opportunity cost! Now if we open our eyes to what's around us we can use this to our advantage so that we benefit from it! We must be the producer to our user; the supply that we demand not just demanding things. In a nut shell, we need Capital to feed our hungry state of existence.

Capital is an asset, money, land, and any resource that generates money. Don't have capital get money to acquire capital! Omar, wait we can't get a loan, the banks won't lend to us. I answer that question with a question. If I were to ask you how the rich stay rich most people would say, ownership (which is capital) and investing! I would follow up with a second question, in the beginning how did many of these huge companies get started? Many people would then say out loud INVESTORS! So, Omar your saying all these terms, telling us to build these assets out of nothing and giving all these history lessons on how companies got started, what does all this truly mean? It means that if we invest in ourselves and neighbors, create and asset to acquire more capital than we would start to establish ownership! That's just one aspect however because remember I said supply and demand so the capital that can produce a service or product is the supply now for it to all work we simply must do what we always do except do it with our own business!! We must be responsible producers and must be responsible customers. Don't go into your local store asking for a deal, pay top dollar to your grocery store so his business can grow to the point where he can buy more in bulk, have finances to hold his inventory, and thus can lower the price, because when you buy in bulk the per unit cost declines therefore making the price decline. To many times African Americans want fruit right after they just planted the seed!

Wait he couldn't say what I think he is saying some unbelievers may ask? Yes, I'm asking us to COME TOGETHER! Please let me let you in on a little secret as well……. come close

People started to push closer to Omar.

most black people don't know because we are so divided…. you ready……. EVERY OTHER RACE HAS BEEN, WILL COUNTINE DOING, AND WILL FOREVER UNITE!!! This concept is nothing knew except to the black people that have just woke up. I know you smell what's burning now, you were just shaking the sleep off and waking up but now I know we got something growing through our bodies, we feel energized, focus, and determined. The adrenalin has finally kicked in.

The crowd praised his words by jumping, embracing on another, throwing fists in the air and shouted Halleluiah!! It wasn't long before we saw three sets of red and blue lights come rolling down. The intercom system echoed disperse, go back into your homes. The crowd roared back with pig and was quickly transforming into a mob. Without a microphone or intercom Omar raised his hands and said silence and made everybody still.

"Officers we were just leaving. I know a great place where we can finish up talking, follow me." Omar announced walking down the street. The stampede of black faces made its way down the street attracting others to join to cure their curiosity. The walk down the blocks seemed like a march or protest and started drawing many police cars along the sides. The law was still intact and left the police just spectating waiting for the chocolate crowd to get out of line. The march ended at the front door of Taylor's restaurant.

Tamie came outside. "How may I help you all?"

"I hope your ovens and stoves are still warm because we are hungry and need a place to gather and talk." Omar said

Tamie's eyes watered as she ran back in the restaurant and said come on.

The air was filled with the aroma of fried legends. Chicken, Catfish, pork chops found its home on the plates ready to be served accompanied with mash potatoes, mac and cheese and corn bread that tasted like cake. Taylors signature BBQ sauce dripped from Ribs and chicken. The sound of Ice smashing against the glass cup sounded with each step of the waitresses alarming the customer of the upcoming beverage. The meals were devoured the second the cook said order ready. It seemed when the meal was done there wasn't a belt buckle unbuckled.

The combined conversations of everyone formed a roar of laughter and commotion. Tamie's eyes could barely hold the tears forming when she approached me.

"Darrius... I mean I don't know what to say!"

"Please don't thank me. It was Omar that lead the convoy here."

"That's funny, I just spoke with Omar and he said that he got the idea to come here from you."

My mind froze, why would Omar tell Tamie that. We hadn't even spoken today and the first time I had even set foot in Taylors joint was earlier today before the meeting. The coincidences of the past accompanied by this most recent started to all tell a story of mystery surrounding Omar.

"Well nevertheless I just pray that everybody is reminded of what we provide here." Tamie said interrupting my thoughts.

"Yes, well judging by everyone's look of satisfaction I feel comfortable saying confidence restored." I said laughing.

The sound of metal hitting glass rang over everyone's conversation as the Muslim lady calmed the crowd. Omar stood up.

"Listen up yall. Our dining experience here has been fulfilling to say the least."

"Fulfilled my next 5 meals" A person in the back shouted across the room as the crowd laughed at the comedian.

"Yes Mr. Taylor sure enough fulfilled everyone. Let me tell you something he has always been here. Mr. Taylor besides Harry's barbershop is the last black owned business in Saints Grove yall. He is a supply to your demand and yet many of yall walk right past this spot to an another fast-food spot or restaurant. Jeff what is the definition of supply and demand?"

"A person and or organization that establishes a product or service that caters to a customer need for a price." Jeff proudly boosted his new-found knowledge.

"Exactly, Brothers and Sisters we have been shoppers for too long. We need to reverse our thinking and plan more for service providers and product producers than consumers. However, when we do consume we must consciously try to nurture our own businesses, and to further grow our own economy. We must look more toward home ownership than home rentals. We must begin to acquire capital to build an asset. I want to give the floor to Mr. Taylor so that he may say a few words."

Mr. Taylor stepped from behind the counter and walked to the center of the building. The fans were working overtime to keep the body heat down in the building. He took out a white cloth and dabbed his forehead.

"I have lived in Saint Groves for over 40 years. Moved here when I was 19 years old stationed in the army. After I got out I moved right there on Jackson street a few blocks up and bought my first piece of land. It wasn't much but it was mine. I met my beautiful wife of 39 years and had a beautiful strong willed daughter. I have worked in the restaurant businesses all my life, cooking for folks. I was a cook in the army. When I got out I busted more tables than there are blades of grass on a football field. Prepared more meals at other restaurants than I can even bare to think off. But all my penny pitching and savings allowed me to buy my own restaurant. This place was more than just a great southern food location. It was a landmark of black enterprise, before my restaurant only a barbershop down the street was owned by a person of color. Harry Gerald Lewis was his name. He too was a town jewel until he got to old and sold it to his son. His son saw the property as a burden and fell in love with the sale price than he did owning his own establishment. He sold it leaving me the last one standing for some time, until his father used his last to buy it back a few years back. I can see that all you youngsters aren't afraid of work and you're not afraid of risk. Many of my peers wouldn't agree, saying that you are lazy and afraid to take chances but I see many of you all up every day in the early morning catching the bus to jobs sometimes coming from one job going to another. I see many of you women raising multiple children by yourself and see to many of you risking your own freedom to indulge or sell drugs and participate in these gang activities. You have your energy misguided you see. Omar may be a stranger you see and that's not a bad thing. I must admit that we have been giving you old teachings of finding a job, stay until retirement but understand I come from a time where just being treated as a human being was a grand obstacle that we overcame. You all however are the evolution with new obstacles to conquer. We as a people must free ourselves from these corporate giants and begin building our own empire. We have done enough for everyone else and now I believe it is time to do more for ourselves. I like to thank Mr. Omar for giving us new perspective and opening many of our eyes to not just to what we have been doing wrong but to the opportunity we have to create something big."

The people stood up clapping for Mr. Taylor many of which felt bad for avoiding this place and inspired to do more. After I took my eyes off Mr. Taylor I scanned the room for Omar. I zeroed in on his location heading out of the door.

"Hey Omar" I yelled after him.

"Mr. Darrius great job on bring your guests and on this restaurant recommendation." Omar congratulated.

"Yea about that I never introduced you to my brother and his friends so how did you know their names and I never even spoke of this restaurant to you." I questioned.

"Listen to Psalms 139: 1-3, but in the meantime let me see what you wrote today." Omar said taking my note pad once again fanning through the pages. "Very good work, next assignment. *African American victim sympathy is long forgotten. African American throwing fault at systems and others are all the gossip. Blaming others that do not care has wasted so much precious time and have not aloud that victim to be a survivor and a fault to be an advantage.* I will need that by tomorrow for our next meeting at 7:00 pm and don't worry your wife she will be fine for that night. Oh congratulations by the way."

Before I could open my mouth to ask a ton of questions from his statement Tyson yelled out "Yo Darrius you coming bro or is you going to stay a while."

I turned around and told him I would be right there. When I turned back he was gone. I looked up and down the street for him with no sign. I took a deep breath of the wintery air and made my way to the car.

Once in the car I looked over at Jeff, Tyson and Roger and they looked back each nodding their head in approval for my action to get them here. On the way home, nothing was said. The music was faint like a whisper. We were all digesting not just the delicious food we had but the messages of Mr. Taylor and Omar.

Once I arrived home it seemed the house was dipped in bleach scrubbed clean in the sink. The chrome on the stove was polished to shine like diamonds and the carpet looked like it had just been installed, I could still see the vacuum tracks on the carpet. The air had the aroma of lavender and vanilla almost as if someone was cooking it from the stove. The house was completely baptized and made pure free of all things un cleaned. Candles were lit around the apartment forming shadows that danced on the walls.

"Babe I'm home" I announced as I inspected the house. She stepped out of the bed room stomach first in black laced leggings that swaddled her caramel thighs down to her perfectly formed calves ending in black hills that was polished to shine brighter than the chrome on the stove. Her laced bra and panties looked as if it had been painted on perfectly crafted for her body. Her hair was flawless standing in perfect formation lying flat. Her lips reflected the candle light with her smooth lip gloss. She was perfect leaving nothing to the imagination but still concealing the true sight.

I stepped closer to her with each step arousing me further as I got closer to my lust. I could see the passion in her eyes when I consumed her stomach with my hands.

"How was your meeting?" She asked as if I was really going to interrupt this moment for the lessons I learned. Tonight, was all about catering to my desires! Tonight my black community was prosperous, tonight my black people where free, tonight everything was right as I consumed your tongue inside my mouth kissing her passionately.

We were art in motion the whole night as our bodies satisfied one another, draining each other of all our stress and the last of our energy until the candles had been reduced to puddles of wax and both our bodies doze off into slumber.

Chapter 17

2 Tone

My hands are powdered with dry wall residue and the skin on my knuckles is pulled back with blood dripping from them. The pain is absent because of the adrenalin anger has brought. I clear the table off of any items standing on it to the wall shattering some materials.

"What the fuck is going on" I yelled into the phone

"Niggas isn't answering the phone, cats is having a change of heart, and I swear I see dem boys tailing me and scoping my shit out. I thought you was supposed to make shit easier! "

The voice on the other line has sold me faulty services, and bullshit excuses. He gives me reasons for short comings instead of solutions. This so called street insurance I purchased was supposed to cure all this heat, it was supposed to create smoother business operations.

Worst yet was the fact that the source of my revenue shortage was my very one right hand. I beat the hell out of the first Nigga that threw Roman's name out there whipping his ass for not only for coming up short wit product and funds but for also using Roman as a way out. Shit when Roger came at me with the same story I had to give it some credibility. Roger was wise to say no to a re up on the phone cause I probably would had given him the same ass whoopin. I haven't seen Roger or many other members of my crew for a little while now. Omar is a name that keeps recurring as well, preaching similar shit that Roman be saying before he take them off the block.

I can't even fully bring the hammer down on the insubordination because the police beating down my back. I thought Bone was a lose end but knocking him off ended up opening me up to many accusations and speculation.

I can't believe this shit is what got the pot all stirred up! They act like I invented this hood shit! I was born into it! The whole city won't let this little girl rest in peace with no justice but they passed my sister off as a random act of violence! Black folks want to unify now and do what right but that shit was gone when I was knocking on doors, or when I needed a meal or some clothes. The community didn't give a fuck about me, teachers labeling me a lost cost wit out even attempting to seek, the police targeting me before I even became a Bulls eye. I'm to be damned because I feed the block the only way I know how!

These fuckin cops want justice for one little girl but ignore the hundreds upon hundreds of years of injustice for us. Ali knew what it was and he choose to have his daughter in that spot with the world he lived in. I wouldn't bring my kids to no drug deal, but he brought his daughter to a known trap house and nobody question that shit. Like I had X ray vision and knew she was in there. And I know this Nigga hit Roman's house and he didn't give a damn about his kids! Man fuck Ali and fuck Rome even more. His fam get hit and it's my work that keep his ass safe and it was my world that put the money in his pocket. This Nigga hear a few words from a Nigga name Omar and flip the whole script! And fuck Omar, he don't even live on the block but he feel he can tell my story and say what not to do. And fuck this weak ass Ross because his ass was paid for no damn reason, but I can't complain to his higher ups so I just hang up on his punk ass!

Cordell

The yelling is muted by the disconnection. His punk ass thought I was working for him, like I'm one of his employees. Tone is my worker that pay to keep on working. He does reckless shit with the Intel I give him and he gets mad at me because he has attention with his loud actions. Tone was getting to big to handle anyway, I had to draw out before the feds got noisy. Ali was way more low key and knew how to operate discreetly. He sold the same quality Tone did but for less. Tone knew his business had serious competition so he wildly sprays his house claiming Ali's daughter. Hell I think that bullet did the little girl a favor, now the people can say what she would had been when she got older, a doctor, lawyer and all those other high paying careers. Instead of that little girl growing up to be some bodies baby momma stuck on welfare, or her holding up one of these thug guys so they can mess up the streets even more. My bet would be that she be one of these lose ghetto black girls in the streets.

Truthfully I got nothing against Tone or Ali and I don't give a damn about neither two. They are business deals and deals always expire. Thing about black folks is they talk to damn much and get to damn flashy attracting unwanted attention. I get my cut off them because I put my life on the line everyday with these animals and the department doesn't pay me shit! The shit all gets confiscated and auctioned off anyway and the money goes God knows where so do I feel bad. Hell no. I take another drag of the cigarette and walk back inside.

Ali.

There is a piece of carpet missing from my living room floor and the walls are freshly painted. I filled the holes in the dry wall and replaced the window that shattered. Look like nothing ever happened, a few days ago this place looked like a slaughter house. I actually saw the bullets rip through her body. She didn't cry, she didn't scream, her death was to quick for her to realize what was happening. I took down every picture of her because she just kept staring at me. The funeral home is some blood thirsty Niggas using my grief as a profit charging me all this shit. She worth it though. It's just fucked up I can't even give her an open casket funeral. One of them bullets hit her head. My little girl wouldn't want to be buried anyway. She was a free spirit so ima spread her ashes in the ocean so she can travel to all the places I would had never been able to take her. She usually stayed with my mom but for some reason I wanted her with me that night. Why did I want her there that night? I didn't have anything planned for her, I just don't understand it.

What's so messed up is that I use to justify what I did to take care of her but that lead to bitch made nigga Tone taking her for a dollar. Revenge controls my thoughts, spite controls my heart, and pain is aimed at my adversary. Where the fuck is this Nigga at anyway, he said he had to take a call and went to go smoke but he been gone a minute.

I never trusted this dude but I knew I had to play ball because he invited himself into my business. Offering me cop free streets, and worry free dealing. Corrupt muthafucka must think I'm stupid thinking he looking out for me. He ain't offering me no deal he just leaching off my work. I know he will string me up if he had to and I would do the same. I got myself destruct if it come to it. If I go down ima make sure that pig go down. Detective Ross ain't nothin but a legalize gangsta that hide behind a badge.

"Look Tone is going to be around the church Tomorrow night, your opportunity will be golden to take him out. Me and my partner will be there trying to pull Roman in for questioning so if you have a clear shot take em both out." I will make sure my partner isn't in the area. I will make a false pursuit over the radio so that he come to my back up." Ross says coming back in the house.

"Who was that over the phone?" I asked

"It was Tone I was setting him up for you. Now remember once you're running the product I'm in for 15 percent." He said.

"Yea don't worry you will get what's coming to you."

"Thanks partner it's a pleasure working with you." He said with a smirk.

"Look let's get one thing straight, we aint fuckin partners, and we damn sure aint alliances. We got a common interest to knock off Tone and get this money and that's all it is! You wanted to get me some intel where the fuck where you when them niggas hit my damn house! Where was the intel at then?" I yelled

"Ali I didn't..!"

"Shut the hell up! I'm not in the mood to hear anymore bullshit. We aint got nothing more to talk about tonight. I will see you tomorrow at church." I said walking out of the living room.

Cordell

I get off the couch and walk outside to my car. I slide into the driver's seat already thinking about the money I was going to get. Tone didn't want to share and his 10 percent wasn't satisfying to me like it used to be. Ali's deal is much more lucrative. I allow Ali to speak freely with his words now because I need him to focus on taking out Tone. One thing about niggers is they get emotional and lose track of logical reasoning. His grief is what drives him but it's all about a monopoly to me which means more wealth generation.

Tone was too out of control and Ali wasn't determined enough to make more money. So I had to take matters into my own hands. Puppets where harder to manipulate than these niggers were! All I had to do was tell Tone of possible expansion into Ali's hood and he bit it hook line and sinker. Ali's daughter was never the plan but her death couldn't have made the outcome any better. Ali would kill off Tone, and my hands would be free of blood; all the while these animals will be the ones dripping it from their mouths.

I laugh thinking about the power they thought they had as I sped off into a more desirable zip code leaving the zoo of SG.

Chapter 18

Darrius

The ground was carpeted with a fresh coat of water, puddles gathered along the curb creating tidal waves every time a car drove past. The wind was vocal whistling in my ear as its cold breath took away the feeling from my ears and nose. The cold numb feeling on my face would soon consume my body as a wall of people blocked my view as I approached a populated area in the middle of the street. The cross street was Jackson and 14th a few blocks from my house. Red and blue lights crowded the Christmas lights on the homes as they projected onto the houses around the incident. The sound of the accumulated voices was deafening. I battled with shoulders, elbows and hips fighting my way to front of the crowd. I immediately fell to my knees and let out a piercing shout!!!! Tears joined the rain water as they dripped from my chin to the ground. Fear griped my soul, anger filled my eyes and helpless made me hysterical. The body was exhausted lying stagnant on the icy ground drenched in blood. His clothes were soggy bleached red. The body seemed heavy when the medics lifted him on the stretcher. The absents of any facial expressions or movement made him seem like a manikin, something like an object rather than a person.

Suddenly the crowd froze in movement and muted their words. The lights ceased to illuminate the night and only a street light shined its spot light on me and the corpse that I knew but couldn't identify. I looked around and found myself alone. I looked back at my deceased company only to find him absent. Two head lights appear in the distance creeping closer and closer. I don't move from the middle of the street. I stand glaring right into the lights blinding me further the closer the vehicle approached. The car stops inches away from my body and the door swings open.

"Yo get in bro we late." I couldn't make out the driver; I stepped toward the passenger side of the car and was met with repeated honking!!! It grew louder and louder pounding my ear drums. He began yelling at me, "He's here he's here!"

His words turned into my wife's voice shouting at me, "wake up he's here wake up!" My eyes adjusted to the dim room, I felt the bed shift as my wife rolled over facing away from me still naked from the passion of last night. I was still half sleep thinking of how usually my dreams allows me to take foreign exotic trips to places that reality forbids me from, however this dream seem to take me right outside my door to the street of Saint Groves.

"Babe I think he's coming!" She said swinging her legs off the edge of the bed. When she stood up a waterfall fell on the carpet down her leg. The fluid hitting the fabric of the floor in a sort of thud sound froze us in our poses, both of us grasping what would follow.

"Oh my god my water just broke!" She screamed.

"Okay baby relax let's get you to the hospital." I said with my heart pounding out of my chest. I flew into the kid's room awakening them from their sleep. I threw the first articles of clothing on them I found.

"How you doing in their babe!" I yelled out.

"I'm okay baby, just getting my overnight bag togeethhhhherr. Oooohhhhhhh!!!! She screamed clenching her hands full of sheets leaning on the bed in agony as the contractions stripped away her comfort.

"Get the Damn car now and throw the kids in it!!! She commanded.

I grabbed a pair of sweats and a sweat shirt and stumbled out the door trying to get dress while running out to get the car. The air was cold driving the feeling in my face numb. The air was thick with my breathing as I gasp for the frozen oxygen sprinting to the car. I jammed the key in the ignition starting the car. My face was once again slammed with the cold air hitting my face from the vents! I cranked the heater all the way up and floored the car in reverse and then slamming it into drive giving my own self whip lash. I pulled up to my apartment unit and ran up the steps.

I bust through the door to find my wife and kids struggling to the door, my kids due to fatigue and my wife due to the power of the contractions. She was on the phone with the hospital informing them of her current state. I assisted my family and huddled them in the car and lunched for the hospital.

The heat was finally kicking in as the warm air gave my numb face feeling again. The early morning gave me freedom on the street with the reduced traffic as we broke through Saints Grove jurisdiction to the freeway racing to Tacoma. My wife was breathing frantically struggling to maintain her composer with the contractions. I pulled through the emergency station and off loaded my family.

My wife placed all her support on me as she walked at an angle leaning back on me. The staff immediately supplied us with a wheel chair and she was placed in a room.

The whole early morning was a blur as she transferred custody from doctor to doctor. I remember pacing back and forth in the waiting room angry that I couldn't stand by her. I had to stay with my kids until her mother arrived who was running 10 minutes late to her show time she had given me. I had text a mass message to everyone I could think of for the arrival of my son. I remember hearing the white doors swing open. I turned towards the door expecting my mother in law to be there but instead was substituted with Roman!! "Man, I just got your message cuz where's Chelsea? "

"She in the delivering room!" I said anxiously.

"Man, what you waiting for, go in there I got the kids fam!"

I took his offer and rushed over to the front counter announcing myself as the father and demanding to get in. I remember being thrown a gown, gloves, hair net and mask and guided through the operating doors where the white light was blinding. I found my wife screaming in agony every time the command push was given.

"Push! You're doing good Chelsea you're doing great push!!! The nurse would say.

She waived me over to her position by my wife's side.

"Okay dad I'm going to need you to take my place and hold her hand and encourage her to breath and push when we tell her too" She explained.

"Okay okay!" I said with anxiety.

I grabbed her hand and felt the power of nature as her grip smashed my muscles and crushed my bones in my hand. Sweat gathered at the top of her forehead and began washing all over her face. The sweat on her head created frizzy hair that looked as if a balloon had been rubbing up against it.

"Push!!"

"Aawwwwwwww!!!!! Ooohhh mmmyyy Ggooooddddd, I can't do this, I just can't do this give me the epidural!!!" Chelsea shouted surrendering to her pain!

"We are too far into labor Chelsea, I'm going to need you to be strong and continuing following our instructions and pushing when we say push!" The nurse shouted back.

I was stuck in shock as I was failing at my only job to encourage her. I couldn't find a single word to say to her as she battled with labor.

Her mouth moved but I heard no words. I looked over and saw the medical staff speaking and it was if I was watching a movie with no audio. My thoughts started to drag me deep in them. I remember thinking if it was our intimate session that had been the source of this early labor. My mind further drifted with my nervousness of being a father again. Even though we already had two I didn't want to repeat the same mistakes I had made with them. With this new child I needed to be better. I couldn't be a slave anymore to someone else's empire. Oddly Omar's words began to run throughout my mind. His words of entrepreneurship, capital, asset building, and establishing collaboration with my community controlled my thoughts. Will I have time for my new born and rekindle time with my children or am I destine to continue this dead-end path.

I remember looking at my wife thinking about all this with her screaming in pain. I remember feeling helpless to her needs, it seemed as though she was screaming for help and all I could do was stand by her side. Not hold her up for support but stand by as a witness as she faced her challenges. My thoughts had speed up time as a piercing Sharp cry broke me out of my own selfish thoughts.

"Oh, my he is a beauty" the doctor announced introducing our son to the new world. He was immediately consumed in a blanket and cleaned off. They placed him in a drawer like bed with a light above him that let off heat. His eye lids defended his eyes from the bright light slamming them shut. The towels wiped away the pregnancy fluid from his body.

"8.5 pounds what a big boy, Dad do you want to see your new son" the nurse asked. I walked over and the nurse placed him in my arms. Although his body was light the weight of his present wore heavy on my shoulders and would be on my mind.

For the rest of my day I had to share my wife and children with the whole family and friends that came.

"Man, how you feel cuz?" Roman inquired

"Man, I know this may sound strange but I feel nervous man. Like I don't wanna keep goin this route, like I go back to work in a few days and it's going to be the same shit.

Overtime be draining me but it be so damn expensive that a brutha need overtime just to make rent in time!" I said painfully laughing.

"Man, I feel that, but like Omar said we need to start planting that seed now. We need to own our craft not craft for others and I tell you one thing I let go of that life cuz. Omar is right I can't keep being the infection requesting a cure."

Romans words seemed like another language to me. Was this really the same Roman that use to mock people for playing by the rules. I thought back to all the trouble Roman and I would get into and even though that was years ago, and we had grown up since then this was the first time I notice that he had grown up.

"Real talk though we need to change the way we see and do things, not just us but all of us. I been working hard on the block trying to take the same bruthas I put on, out of the game." Roman said.

Rome and I stayed in the hospital for hours before I had to go run some errands. Chelsea had plenty of family there and gave me her blessing to go. On the car ride I broke the silence of the ride.

"Man, I feel this whole change of heart to the streets but you need to be careful, you taking cats off the block reduces revenue for the people they work for and hell aren't you and 2 Tone partners, or use to be partners?"

"Yup you got it right the first time. We are and always will be partners and that is why I'm not leaving him behind." He said and almost as if we had rehearsed the conversation and timed it with a scene changed we had pulled into 2 Tones place of residence. I had been so engulfed in our conversation that I didn't recognize the familiar territory.

The smooth pavement had turned into gravel the pop rock like sound of our wheels rolling over the little rocks announced our presence to the people inside. The lawn had patches of grass with dirt representing the majority of the lawn. The house was painted in a light blue that had been transformed to ashy blue due to the peeling of the paint. He had a new white front door that seemed out of place on the dingy looking house. Rumor has it someone kicked his previous door down trying to rob him a few months ago, there was three men already outside when we pulled up.

"What up Rome" one greeted.

"What's good fellas" Roman replied.

The position of their pants and the way their shirt protruded out accompanied by their posture told me that they were armed. I didn't even know why we were here or why we would stop here right after my son was born.

2 Tone must have felt our presence because he walked outside.

"Shit if aint my nigga Rome and Darrius" 2 Tone Announced.

Roman reached behind his back and pulled out a Glock 40 out of his waste banned alarming the three fellas around him. Each one of them responded with pulling out their weapons. My hands flew up in a surrendering stance. Dead silence consumed the standoff as Roman held his gun tight by his side and the other men pointing their weapons at Roman.

"The fuck you doin nigga!" One of the men replied.

"Giving it all back." Roman said as he released his magazine dropping it and racking the bullet in the chamber out of the weapon following the magazine to the ground. Roman then tossed the unloaded gun at 2 Tone's feet.

"The fuck that dramatic shit supposed to mean?" 2 Tone demanded.

"It means I'm out, but I didn't come here just to tell you that I also came here to take you with me. We aint gotta do this shit any more. This life is something we don't even want our kids in. This life always had us looking over our back and we messing up our own community and causing these otha youngsters to follow in our footsteps." Roman responded.

"You know, niggas was telling me you went 360. But damn nigga I didn't know you was this far gone. I heard you think you this random nigga disciple and shit preachin on corners about stop the infection. Who the fuck you think you is?" 2 Tone said laughing with the three other men joining in!

"So your gonna stand there and act like you don't see what we doin. You gonna stand there and act like this position don't have an expiration date. Look we ran the streets and did what we felt we had too, I get it but we know other ways now! There's a movement going on Tone and what we doing holds things back. We cant keep infecting our community like this. Look man we both know the messed up shit we did and the only way the lord will show us mercy is if we repent and change."

"You see that's the shit I'm talking about. Talking about merciful God this and merciful God that! Hell, I hope he at least is merciful because he surely isn't fair!! All my life I heard niggas condemn people like me who survive in this unbalanced world! These white cats are out here running downhill while us street niggas running up hill with a ball and chain. So I think it would be right if God at least had mercy on a nigga for not being able to keep up. You gonna judge me like we don't see the same shit! A doctor, lawyer, Governor, veterinarian, and shit like that is in my blind spots!! The only thing God put in my view is these streets and these streets is a battle field!! God birthed a soldier the moment he put me in my moms! You see the white folks give us the test before they even give us a book or a lesson! So fuck it! If they set me up to fail, then they encouraged me to cheat and if going against this legal corruption with illegal survival then so be it!"

"Thats exactly what I'm trying to get you to see! You see only the flaws in your life and your questioning God as if he owes you an answer. You have been so consumed with justifying your actions making society be the villain and you're only a victim trying to survive by poisoning your own community. Success from the destruction of others makes you just as corrupt as the white people you point the finger at."

"Shit I just don't point the finger at white people, I also point it at hypocrites like you! The people in this game choose to be here! I didn't draft anybody in this game. Niggas see a way to get it and choose up just like one would do for a college, job or any other option! How am I to blame for somebody who seeks me out and purchases my product completely voluntarily! That's free will nigga, u like free will when cats are giving money to the church or doing so called good but free will is suddenly bad when they choose a path that don't go in the direction of your compass. You call it success by corruption I call it prosperity by conquering! To be honest yall religious origins have been more corrupt, claimed more lives and have divided more nations than a nigga like me will ever do! It's about time yall stop being stupid telling me to wake up when yall the ones selling dreams, these white folks have been building their empires off minority backs since the beginning of time and they still the elite class! Obviously, God must have chosen to give them their heaven now and ours hopefully later! Nigga I've been a wake for a minute now you must have fallen asleep talking that shit you talking."

"If all you see is a nightmare, then how do you expect to see any opportunity? You not only see it but you deny it. If I showed you a new path you would close your eyes and cover your ears and that is you not using your freedom of choice because you deny your options only leaving these streets. The non-legitimate way to make this money appears to be ideal because its fast money. Brutha listen just because the ligament way may take longer and have many obstacles don't mean you can't do it. These police are crackin down out here and it's only a matter of time before you get caged up or somebody knock you off." Roman Pleaded

The bystanders paused in there posture, even the weather seem to have stop its actions to listen. 2 Tone was dead silent eyes seem to be cutting right through Roman. Roman lifted up his hands and announced he was done which shock 2 Tones loyal foundation. Roman had been 2 Tone's right hand man and just like many other people in his life Roman was leaving him behind.

"Nigga you got the game twisted if you think you can just put yo damn two weeks' notice in and think that there won't be consequences! You forget that niggas lit up yo moms spot the otha day and you think them otha niggas is just gonna stop comin for you! You think you can just roll up to my spot and disrespect me with your dismissal of my life and you just go unchecked! This ol preachin ass nigga Omar need to understand that I don't give a damn about him but when his so called church flood my business then that's where we got a problem and you already know how I deal wit problems! Ima let you chill on that for a sec and hopefully you come to yo senses because if not then you just like every otha nigga in the streets to me. And Darrius you neutral ground and all but if you roll wit your cuz again when he talking that bullshit then you may catch one too! Because I would hate for Chelsea and yo kids to be alone in this world!

In that second the weight of my family that I usually carried to drive me to get through another day became the fuel that ignited my anger. I immediately broke through my submissive peace keeping demeanor and exploded with rage at his threat to my reason for existence!

"What the fuck you say nigga! Don't you put none of mine in your damn mouth again! My wife and kids might as well be forbidden words!" I hollered advancing towards 2 Tone.

Roman invaded my opportunity to get closer to him holding me back and screaming get back in the car.

"Yea that fam struck that nerve huh choir boy. All that turn the otha cheek shit and live in peace went bye bye! Just know this Darrius and Roman yall got history wit me and is the only reason why I aint have my fellas blow yo heads off. So instead of giving your loved ones a closed casket funeral to attend ima give yall some advice. The way you felt when I threaten to mess up your fam is what I feel when mess wit my business messing up my way of living for me and mines! Just how you was ready to take it there expect the same shit from me. Now get the hell of my property before I changed my mind!

Feeling defeated we both retreated to the car. The gravel shifted under the wheels as we backed out of Tones drive way and shoot down the road. Even though the wind was cold with the windows down I was hot from anger and fear of his threats. Roman however seemed not only calm but focus. His left hand was tight on the steering wheel while his right hand rested on the driving lever even though it wasn't a stick shift.

"Man why the hell did you do all that? You up here actin like you invincible. Bru Im happy that your moving your life in a positive direction but man you still can't forget where you at. This is SG and you can't just go to drug dealer's spots and charge them up like that even if you grew up with them! 2 Tone isn't Andre anymore Rome!" I explained

"So what you saying Darrius! Just because he isn't dressed in his Sunday best, or is a harmless elderly person he isn't worth trying to reach! It's that thinking that got many of these leaders and so called educators giving up before they even try to reach some of these cats out here. Omar said that we as a community need to wake up and them people whether you like it or not are a part of it! So, don't try and talk about some selective teaching shit because I'm not for that!" Roman rebutted.

His words had me stuck in silence. By all counts Roman could not have been more right and I felt like a coward at best! My mind took me back in time when I swore to defend my nation from all enemies. When I was deployed in the dessert I wouldn't have hesitated to fire off at anyone if given the command and yet I found myself fearful to even reach out to someone I had grown up with.

"Look you right man you right, but check it 2 Tone is stuck in his ways and to be honest I would expect that, I mean them saints Grove streets raised him and this life is all he knows so to just shoot a do better speech at him and expecting him to change his whole way of thinking is unlikely so in irony his response to rebuke what you were trying to say is considered normal but you are a phenomenon. I mean I was there when you first heard Omar and ever since that night you have done a 360 off one 30-minute speech in which you argued with him for a good amount of that time. So, I say all that to ask what really happened bruh."

Roman glanced at me and while smiling recited" *You have searched me, Lord, and you know me. You know when I sit and when I rise; you perceive my thoughts from afar. You discern my going out and my lying down; you are familiar with all my ways.*"

"What is that?" I asked

"The shots that landed on my house a few days ago created more havoc than anybody will ever know?"

"What you talking about, I mean I know your mom was hot and all and LaShandria isn't your biggest fan and yo young one was scared but everyone one was safe. Plus I'm sure that's not the first time you had a bullet flown your direction."

"Nobody did get hurt. I mean how could a person that never took their first breath be hurt or killed for that matter."

My eyes darted at roman and saw his calm focus demeanor flow from his eyes. My mind darted back to LaShandria's short comment and her expedited travels up the stairs to her room. I immediately remembered Roman pouring the burning fluid down his throat! The way he had glared at me when I said thank god no one got hurt. The signs that were blind to me before were crystal clear in my memories.

"She was pregnant? How come you didn't tell nobody?" I asked.

"Because yall would have missed the beauty in new life! Rome how you gonna support another baby, Rome you not even married yet, Rome you bearly take care of the one you got now and that other shit! Man everyday I went out on dem streets and risked my freedom for my family. I didn't know of this shit Omar is dishing out now. True I have not been able to give my kids what they deserve but I love the hell out of them and it's not one single day I wouldn't give up my life for them which is what I did every single day hustlin." Rome was trying desperately to capture all the tears pouring down his eyes with his shirt. "Damn this!" He said swerving off the road and slamming his foot through the break causing me to choke on my seat belt and smash back into my seat! He unbuckled his seat belt and got out the car. We on the side of the over pass and he walked over to capture the view. I exit out the car and joined him on top of the world, the wind seemed cooler at the height we was at but the view was spectacular.

"It was about 11 at night when my house got lit up. I was chillin with Rome on the block picking up some money when my mom's called about them blastin. She told me she heard the bullets hit the house when she hit the ground crawling to the kitchen to get my heat from under the sink. When I finally got off the phone wit her I Jetted to the car and told Tone to gas it all the way there. I remember me being hot man. Even tho it was cold as hell outside. I remember I looked at my crib when I got there and seeing my girl and daughter shock beyond fear! She was holding my daughter so tight that I couldn't see if she got hit. Man all I could think about is that little girl on the news! All I could think about was my karma! When I finally got to examine her I realized she was physically okay but then I looked at Lashandria's stomach and wondered about the baby. A few days later I forgot that karma doesn't forget, I made love to her bro just like we did back in the day, I mean she was pregnant and all but we still got it done. I wake up to her crying and she jump up and run to the bathroom, the door was closed and locked. I told her to open it but she wouldn't. I could hear her huffing and puffing and sniffing her nose crying. I kept saying open the door. She still wouldn't do it bruh. So I step back and kicked that shit in and I found her lying in the tub field with blood and blood all over the walls from her hands finger painting. I said where the fuck the blood come from! Where you bleeding! She told me she couldn't hold him so she choose to sit with him! She looked up me and asked why God takes the innocent! I grabbed her from the blood bath bruh and wrapped a towel around and held her until we fainted from exhaustion. She hasn't really spoken to me since and I wanted so bad to blame the miscarriage on dem shots, because I know that stress had to be overwhelming But man it was me." Rome told his story

"Rome don't do that; don't put that weight on you!" I interrupted.

"Be real Darrius, I confide in you because you real with me so don't stop now! I had been stressing her out, my life style, cats gunnin for me; she can't even go out sometimes because my debt could be paid with her life! Dem bullets that found my house that night was only the cherry on top!" Rome interjected.

"Look you can't take responsibility for dem dudes firing those shots at yo house. A lot of spots get shot up it's just how the SG is. The south Tacoma boys been at war with the cats on this end for a while now especially since that girl caught a bullet."

"Man they returned the bullet Darruis! The burner that fired off the bullet that killed her is down there in the water!"

My heart stopped beating as his admission of guilt hit me.

"What you mean by that Rome! Tell me you had nothin to do wit that! Tell me that you just know the nigga that shot or somethin."

Rome looked over at the skyline. The sun was setting and with no clouds in the sky it gave the heavens a milky orange, cherry blueberry swirled look. He analyzed the sky before he looked back at me.

"The bullet wasn't met for her. Me and Tone and our other homie Bone rolled out there. We had found out who robbed Tones house. The hood told on the young cats that carried it out so we knocked them around asking who put them up to this because shit wasn't nobody stupid enough in our hood to do that so we knew it was some out of town shit. Anyway, come to find out a rising cat named Ali In the ST paid the lil homies to do it. So we got word of a joint he hung at and started raining on em. We all started firing off shots! Man I don't know who's bullet hit her but it might as well have been mine. Shit we zipped out of there and rolled right here where we through the weapons in the water. Man I didn't find out to the next day on the news of ol girls death. I knew my karma was coming but that's just that, I thought it was my karma not my unborn child!"

I stared of at the scenery speechless at what had been revealed to me. I knew the only reason why I didn't feel pure disgust with him was because he was my blood. Even though I understood what Rome did in the streets I guess I just choose not to see the blood thirst of the individuals causing the blood shed. The hood is always considered a quote on quote cool place some even wearing it as a mark of honor until it claims one of your own then it becomes the source of demise. My Speechlessness aroused Rome to keep his confessional going.

"With all the shit that go down here I used to think God turned a blind eye to us. Like this shit went unnoticed. I mean we shout it out in rap songs, glamorize it in the movies, I mean damn we showing the world what its really like and yet this shit still go on. That was the way I thought until that night after the police left my spot I drove by and saw sign on the church down the street from Taylors restaurant that read Psalms 132 verse 1-3. Don't ask me why I looked it up because I couldn't tell ya. But it read that quote I said in the car on the way here. I thought nothing of it until I went with you to Omar's spot. His words confirmed that passage bro and man I aint neva been the same since. So much so that I ignore the anger of betrayal Lashandria did. The night she miscarried was the night she moaned Tones name when we was making love. Dog I wanted so bad to kill her and him but my hands have so much sin and blood on them that I couldn't find myself to confront her. She think I don't know but I do. Tone think he hindin something but I know, but I still have to forgive because I'm requesting redemption and forgiveness for my wrong."

The shock of Bones related death and Lashandria's night with Tone raddled me with the mystery of Omar. At this point I recalled Omar quoting that same passage he had told me not to read but listen too. Once again how did he predict the future? How did he know that I would have to listen to the passage instead of reading it? As I thought deeper I also couldn't see how He knew that my Son would be born early in the morning. Based on his congratulations I assumed that's what he meant and that comment about her being fine don't worry was due to her parents being there caring for her and the kids at the hospital. I was snapped out of trying to determine if Omar was some sort of alien when Roman informed us of our running behind our time schedule.

"Look stop worrying about what people is doing to you, stop trying to find out stuff that's out of your control and like I told Tone it's not your position to question the creator. That's why you, me and many othas can't get out of our situations because we not focused on what we can do. We accept the titles and not only fulfill them be grow in them making it more than a title but an identity. Tone may have grown to far in this street life. Many people in this community may never come together to create financial independence, own our craft, turn our hoods into a village of prosperous people, but I can't control that Darrius so I only worry about what I can do to help this situation and know that I am not alone. All that passage means Darrius is that God has been, is, and will forever be with us, but he can only be seen with the glasses of optimism, pure intentioned, positive thinking but not with the glasses we only see this messed up world we think we live in. Shit many of us see defaced property when I see art on one of the best restaurants in town Taylor's Soul. People see those words on that church bill board and I see Gods acknowledgement of his presence in this community. You think I don't think about where Omar came from? You think I haven't notice some unexplained actions? But it doesn't matter, he's here now and has brought these powerful messages that has changed my life and many others and hell if all I got to do is repeat his words to others than that's my role."

We sat for a while on that over past in each other's presents without words. Each one of us in our own thoughts about our lives thus far. I took out my little note pad I had been keeping, documenting my writing assignments. As I looked over the darken sky light up by the Tacoma skyline. I wrote:

Many times when preparing for a fight the African American measures their opponent to the extent that he for gets to measure himself. As we continue to view the white man as the all-powerful and privilege we in essence idolize them telling ourselves that they are on a whole other playing field that we can't compete in. In doing that we also see others like them as enemies before we even know their name. We are fighters expecting to loss and fighters seeing everyone else as a fight. With this mind set The African American has condemn themselves to victims due to their obstacles and because of their division amongst each other they don't help one another there for rendering us helpless. Until the African American sees their neighbor as allies, until the African American feels not only an urge but a sense of responsibility to help their neighbor, Until the African American stops licking their wounds so that they can heal, Until the African American stops seeing less of their opponent and more of themselves will we as a people become prosperous.

I click the pen back into its capsule and could feel the eyes over my shoulder looking at what I had written. I started to open my mouth to explain when he put his hand up.

"Bruh no need to explain, just make sure you get them words in front of many eyes, its about time for us to head over"

As we pulled off from our confession ground I knew Rome had arrived at another level. His eyes had truly been opened to the world around him. I kept thinking back to the dream I had this morning and the fear I had experience. I felt the dream and Rome were somehow connected. Rome wasn't going to stop until the whole town was saved. He saw something bigger than himself which was the idea of the black man truly being free. Free of all the negative stereotypes and second citizen class standards. He wanted the black man free from their financial chains and wanted to end the outside world dictating the pay rate, the laws and policies of lands they didn't live on. Roman had woken up.

Chapter 20

Darrius

We arrived at a colony of people stretching all around Taylor's Soul restaurant. The turnout was unbelievable to the humble beginnings of having these gatherings in Omar's small living room. The audience had gathered from all parts of the community and the air seem to hold so much enthusiasm from the crowd. Most of these individuals you couldn't get to come to church on Easter Sunday so it was a true symbol of progress of our people here to listen to some one speak on the wellbeing of the black community. The spectators started to chant Wake up, Wake up, Wake up! Me and Rome squeezed our way to the front of what I now saw was a stage. I scratched my head wondering when and how he was able to put the platform together. The night was cool but the body heat seem to elevate the temperature. As I looked up the street I saw that it was blocked off just how they would do a block party. The excitement was breath taking. The power of multiplication I thought, each person was always tasked with inviting a few more and than those people a few more to the point where Omar drew a crowd as big as this one. They wasn't here for a concert, government assistance, black Friday or the new Jordan's that came out; they were here for knowledge, ownership and most of all freedom!

Omar appeared on the stage and stepped up to the microphone. He raised one hand to silence the crowd and with a thunderous voice he said.

Omar

WAKE UP! Wake up BLACK SURVIVOR!

It's your fault!!!!!! Not the police that stops you unjustly, the rough neighborhood you lived in, the prejudgment of your character due to the complexion of your skin, the negative stereotype of the black people that have even other black people move away from their own in search of a better life. It's your fault!!!!!! Not the low-income state that denied you certain privileges, the incarcerated parent, the drug induced parent, the single parent house hold with no supervision to help you grow and mature and steer you the right way!!!!! It's your fault!!!!! Not the child you had young, or your lack of education you possess, the low paying job that turns living comfortable into living just to work another day. It's your fault!!!

We have forgotten what we are capable off. We have forgotten the perseverance, toughness and determination that runs through our veins. God gives you everything you need to make it in this world, and if a degree, a perfect no obstacle having life, unlimited resources was what it took to truly survive then we would be born with it. You have the tools hell more tools than most. A lot of people don't have the drive to create financial independence because they have never been hungry, a lot of people don't have the discipline to go without a luxury to receive something better because they have never been without. A lot of people don't have knowledge of responsibility that is had when a single mother or father care for a child because they have never had to be responsible for themselves! You have the drive, discipline that's already in you due to your obstacles and it's your responsibility to bring them out! No more excuses, finger pointing, justifications it's time to WAKE UP!!!!

The crowd echoed after him *"Wake up, wake up, wakeup!"* Chanting is now famous slogan. I felt the power of the crowd finding their inner spirit. Omar took a step back from the microphone. The audience was roaring. I forgot the community held this many people. Omar put his hands up to settle the sea of people then started back again.

"We are blindsided with fear and reside inside the house, never attempting to go out and venture. We settle for government and corporate shelter and down any ideas of journeying into business ownership. We all too often broadcast that fact that starting up businesses has a 90 percent failure rate or that starting a business will drain all you have worked for. We avoid risk and to avoid risk means to find the cure to success. Avoiding risk will relieve the symptoms of greatness and ambition, avoiding risk will reduce the reward of owning an institution and increase the bondage employers will have on your life. We as a people have become numb to opportunity that gives us a chance to escape what Robert Kiyosaki labels the Rat Race. We refuse to invest in our selves placing a cheap price on ourselves, time, worth and a high price on retail goods! We can locate the money to fund a college education that doesn't grantee a prosperous high paying career or even a job for that matter but we can't scrape a penny to build an asset that will make us financially independent!

Wake Up!!!!!! You mean we as a people will lease a new model car, spends thousands of dollars a year on cosmetics, Jordan's, and other brand name items but if an individual offers their neighbor a chance to work independently or invest in a business opportunity we shoot it down in a split second and then have the nerve to call it a pyramid scam or unnecessary risk. I will put out a disclaimer however, there are pyramid type organization and get rich quick scams. At the same time, I know people that can spot a knock off Jordan or Nike shoes in a heartbeat by verifying certain attributes and characteristics on a product, they do complete research. We take time to examine a product that is feeding a corporate giant that will not share its wealth with you and we spend no time even doing research on a product, service or program that can offer them financial independence!! Hell I will say this, before you call any business opportunity a pyramid scheme just take a look at your own employment papers.

We are late to a meeting for a business opportunity but break every traffic law to get to their bosses employment! Why! Its comical how people at the bottom of a corporate pyramid calls everything out side of trading time for money a pyramid! The people we receive advice from about the top of a mountain only know the ground level, we allow them to be our career and entrepreneurial advisors and they don't know how to even direct their own lives!"

The crowd uniformly agreed all nodding and shouting preach brother preach.

"For the African American, the Price that incarceration cost is paid with potential, ambition, self-empowerment and ownership, and due to the rising interest of confinement it requires more of every generation.

The African American people has been caged! That's not even the worst part, we have been confined for so long that we don't even feel claustrophobic anymore! We are comfortable in this societal penitentiary. Freedom is being stripped away in our black communities in Seattle. 35.7 percent of the prison population is embodied by the African American population despite only representing a mere 7 percent of the population. Although these numbers are alarming the bars I'm speaking of are not always made from iron or steel, no the restrictions of our mind and ambition has been placed upon us. We don't have a glass ceiling preventing our growth because having glass overhead assumes that we could at least see high levels of success, we have instead cemented our ceiling. Most African Americans don't even think about the possibility of money working for them only working for money. A slave to this hourly wage system.

Abraham Harold Maslow was an American psychologist who establish Maslow's hierarchy of needs theory. This theory has five stages physiological, safety, love and belonging, esteem and self-actualization. Maslow's Theory places us in survival mode, the bottom of the pyramid. As previously stated Maslow's hierarchy illustrates 5 levels of human satisfaction from basic needs to personal enlightenment. The foundation of the pyramid is Physiological needs, which is the basic factors needed for survival. Food, water and shelter has consumed all our attentions. Many blacks look at a job for their ability to pay rent, buy groceries and pay basic bills only.

Safety is the next level that humans look forward to and is all too many times not achieved. The violence that plagues our communities with drugs, gangs, fear of law enforcement and domestic violence has stripped the protective comfort offered in more established communities. We instead make do with the hostel environment and work with it.

Love and belonging is the third step in in the hierarchy which is only found in subsections of the African American community. We as a people have become so divided that we belong to our certain peer group instead of the collaborative people. West side, south end, old school new school, religious group street group. To add further burden to black unification the subgroups prejudge the other group many times more negatively than positively. Church goers are portrayed as hypocrites or judgmental by the street groups and the street population is met with the blaming reason why the black reputation has become so deteriorated. Old school believes that the youth has lost there way, that the meaning of hard work is a lost definition. The "give me" generation they call us. The youth believe that the old-school generation doesn't understand, it's not the same, that they are stuck in their old ways. We have surpassed their knowledge base they believe which is why we as a people keep repeating a cycle of self-oppression. These different groups look to members that look their same direction and do not unionize everyone's view point to from a 360 analysis.

The next level is Esteem! This level can be tricky because to most African Americans their image is strong, aggressive, stylish, charismatic and beautiful. Just look on these social media platforms that has everyone looking casket sharp in a dead career. The population lives through the few that have made it, Obama as the first black president, athlete stars, entertainment artiest, and past civil rights legends forgetting that the majority is living through a few. Respect is given where you're from and what block you represent in a location where your ownership is absent and in many cases your rent is behind. Numbers show that we only own 1.7 percent of business in Seattle 70 percent only employing 4 people or less! We have high self-confidence on a social network where hundreds and thousands endorse our ego on a post but can't find a cosigner to endorse you on a loan. There is a fine line between popularity and fame. You stick in one town for years you will become popular; however, a stranger can come to your town for a day during a football game and break every record and he will have fame in your city.

Self-actualization is the tip of the mountain in Marlow's theory. Many people black, white, Hispanic, Asian, pacific islander, Indian, native American, foreign or domestic, man or woman, heterosexual or homosexual will never discover this level. This level maxis out all black cards and cash put together and can only be paid with building a legacy of true greatness. It's not paid with finances its only method of payment is your life, the potential that was fully explored. Due to the Black community settling, this level is missed by majority of our people.

So, what does this mean? It translates into the Black community being experts at surviving, knowing the welfare system in and out, becoming pros at dodging creditors, and consuming things that satisfy the material need. For those *that have generated financial success we have become pros at relocating from our less progressive communities to more prestigious where the complexion of your neighbors grow lighter. They are pros at disassociating themselves from childhood friends because hey you show me your five friends and I show you who you are. I will say it again we are PROS at survival!!!!! On the contrary however as a people we are rookies to safety, we are rookies to love and belonging, we are rookies to self-esteem and self-actualization might as well be in heaven because many of us don't believe we can achieve this stage in this life time."*

The crowd echoes wake up, wake up wake up as his words alarm everyone of our current position. Roman is fired up chanting louder than anyone. My eyes are widen with my mind even wider. Omar and Rome where preaching the same message with different words. Ali, Bone, Tone, Lashandria, Rome, Chelsea and me have many reasons to leave some one behind but we ignore all the reasons to help one another out! That's what caused Bones death, Tones pain that spread throughout the community, Romans losses, Lashandria's pain, my disconnection from my family. Its time we looked at our neighbor as a force to join instead a force to challenge my force.

The rest of the night was a festival of proud black motivation. I didn't stay for the fun that night and instead Roman and I found our way back home to where I turned in early. With my in laws watching my kids I got some much needed rest because my vacation had come to an end and it was back to the fields for me.

Chapter 21

Darrius

Tonight, I don't dream. My head rests on my goose down pillow seeping in the feathers causing the ends of the pillow to hug the sides of my face pressing against my ears. The rest of my body pours into the marshmallow soft bed forming to my body. The blanket devours all trapping my body heat against its fabric. The fan blows perfect wind that dances over my face and breaks the awkward silence of the night. The room is dark with lights roaming about my wall when cars drive by. My wife is still at the hospital with our children. My kids get to miss school and my wife won't be going back to work for the next 6 weeks. My vacation ends however, I ran out of vacation hours and must start from scratch laboring for more vacation time to spend with my family. The work day ahead makes me feel so fatigue physically but runs my mind so much that it keeps me awake. Where did my time off go? I look at the clock on my dresser, 2:00 am it reads. 3 more hours till launch. I turn back over realizing how I devoted my whole life too this slaving for a dime. Before Omar I guess I had become numb to me repeating this live to work cycle. Omar's words these past days brought feelings of pain. Damn being asleep was the only thing keeping me sane but now that I am awake the thought of punching in another hour was driving me crazy! I can't go to sleep I just can't!! I can't go to the ocean, mountains, beaches, anywhere! The alarm sounds, damn 6 am already, I got to wake up.

My movements are in auto pilot this morning, doing the same routine by muscle memory not even thinking. Shower, brush teeth, eat one of the kids pop tarts, put myself in dress compliance and go out the door to school.

The parking lot is full again once I get on campus, I have to park in the neighboring apartments and prey that my car doesn't get towed while I learn how to be some else's employee for more money.

I see Alisha. She still has the same braids in last time I saw her. We have a test coming up and I can see the struggle in her eyes. She has a huge course load this quarter and unlike the other privilege kids that study there interests Alisha studies what she think will get her the best paycheck. Classes like theater, political science, and early childhood education is what many in our class major in, they want to make a difference and with people like us it makes no difference. We are interested in being stable; our career goes by the top hiring professions. The medical field is too crowded. Everyone wants to be a nurse. Being a lawyer takes too long, she has a few years at best with staying with her folks, engineer is not on her scale so she thinks, her small local college degree cannot compete with the more expensive private college graduates who's application would accompany hers to the job opening. No the field to go into is business. Its general and she will be able to find steady employment.

I take a seat next to her and skip my usual banter with her and get right to the point with her.

"I want you to go with me some where tonight." I asked.

"Well hey to you too, and I don't think I can. I have way too much homework to get done plus we have a test coming up but besides all that where do you want to take me. Last time I checked you was married." She said with a smirk.

"No it's not like that, I need you to come to a rally tonight. It's going to be about black ownership and entrepreneurship and as for your homework I know you don't have a job so do your work after class before I pick you up, trust me you're not going to want to miss out on this."

As if I was her parent giving her an order she agrees. I didn't follow anyone of the teacher's words the whole school day. I day dream the whole class period about Omar's words trying to put it all together in how it relates in my life. The school bell rings releasing its student hostages.

Stone

"What's up man where you been, I have somebody of interest in the case. I'm going to talk to Roman, there is supposed to be some kind of rally at the local church, it's a perfect time to catch him. These streets seem to be eating every valuable lead so I'm not going to let this one get away." I say into the phone.

"I have to do something, I will explain later. Ima go to the store right quick and hit you when I get back, I have to go follow up with a witness." He answered.

"What witness? You never told me about any witness, we supposed to be partners." I shot back.

"Well some of us are too busy working old case files and not keeping up with the work load."

"It has only been a few days and it was a murder!"

"A few days here is old news compared to all the crimes that keep happening on a daily basis." Cordell responded

I hated how he had a point. In the SG crime is such a tradition that it has lost its value as being sickness of life to it being the norm, almost like getting a cold it's just not a big deal.

My curiosity of his where about were satisfied and felt relieved that he had taken the liberty to do some work on some of our new cases. I came up with an excuse to get off the phone because I needed to play music to keep me up driving. I grew tired on my journey back to the SG, I seemed to be intoxicated with fatigue. I was supposed to go visit the hospital with my new family but had to stop home to recharge for a minute. I never really understood why I had felt so tired that day. I think about it all the time. The day grew old and the night young and gave me a few hours to nap before I would head of to the event. I pulled into the station, set the alarm on my phone and dozed off.

Darrius

I scramble to my car to hurry up and wait in traffic. My moral declines the closer I get to my clock in location as I pull into a crowded parking lot. I feel this is going to be a busy day. I find a parking spot and take a deep breath as I get ready to enter into my new reality for the next 9 hours. I walk in and my thoughts have been verified, the place is flooded with customers.

I fall in line and start answering orders, apologizing to customers for not holding up to their expectations, and catering to the customer's lack of knowledge by going through every inventory item in the store. I used to do all of this with the biggest grin on my face. Many times, customers would comment how much I seem to love my job and one day I will be manager of this store. I had just discharged out of the military when I landed this job so my Sir's and Ma'ams were through the roof and drove my stores clientele crazy. They adored when I would cater to their needs and stroke their egos. On this day however I have been getting displeased looks all throughout the work day. On my ten minute break I go to the restroom, as I wash my hands I look in the mirror and see my reflection so hurt that it was painful to look at. I had aged, I had eyes of a manikin looking as if I had no soul. My expression was defeated and exhausted looking. At that moment I had realized that I didn't put on my customer service mask today, today I wore my true face.

Omar's words of inspiration and encouragement of a better life had motivated me so much that I felt so displeased with this job. I thought back at how unappreciative these customers were and how uncaring my management staff had been. I thought about the receipt snatching money throwing, customers. The micro-managing mangers that only wanted to make quota and when they fell short the failure was placed on my shoulders. I splashed water on my face and walked back out onto the floor. My other coworker Lisa had just clock in. Even though I was only gone a week a lot had changed with Lisa.

Lisa has a good enough mentality. She believed a small roach infested apartment was a castle with company, she believed her 4 dollars above minimum wage was a salary to be envied. Every time a coworker found a problem and asked who did this she naturally assumed it was her. She viewed herself as strong, built for taking punches from others but felt her strength was too weak to throw her own fists. Lisa had a huge capacity to hold loads of people's frustration and anger which only made room for little aspiration. Maybe that was why her ambition was severely limited. What many considered a starting point she thought as the ideal result. Her sense of optimism was almost crippling in a sense of not allowing her the will to fight when things slammed her. She spaced out many times during her work day and drew pictures. I can tell by her long concentration on what she was creating that she was escaping momentarily as I do frequently with my day dreaming. The chains of her reality imprisoned her physically and financially, so her mind had to take to the canvas with whatever utensil was available on what every writing source that could hold ink.

After the day crew left it was usually me and Lisa left closing out the day. I would always inquire on how things were going. She always smiled during her work day but the story of her harsh reality always baffled me how she could wear such a mask all the time. Her mother was losing her war with cancer, her stability of living with her mother was coming to an end as medical bills, debt, and usual household bills consumed her entire government allotment. The wage she brought home wouldn't support herself in the expensive Seattle economy. Her first start in the adult world was already burying her alive. From a financial stand point she never even stood a chance. She represented numerous young black adults in the world running a race from the seats in the stadium. How could they begin from the starting line like other races are privileged to start from? How could she see the true potential of her power when all that surrounds her is mediocrity? Her doubt in herself grew from the environment she came from.

As she continued about how things were going she must have seen my deep concentrated expression because she had halted her story to inquire about what was on my mind. Just like in class with Alisha I invited her to hear Omar speak tonight. She stood there staring at me for a moment before she asked who is Omar.

"It's not so much who he is, it's what he has to say that can really open your mind." I responded.

"What are you talking about Darrius, I am very open minded and expressive, I vent to you every time I have a problem here." She defended.

"By talking behind someone's back about how they treat you? That's not being expressive or standing up for yourself. You just deal with the shit that the world throws at you and do nothing to clean it up! You do all this in the name of being grateful and humble saying that your grateful of what you have, when in reality you are so unsatisfied. Your just like all these black people in the community that have gotten use to starving. They have gotten so used to ignoring their hunger that we call our dreams false hunger pains. We prepare large feast for other corporations with our labor and we find it fulfilling to lick the plates of whatever is left over! You're not open minded because a true open minded person would never except this bullshit!" Before I could censor myself I had already said it. I saw the newly painted expression of sadness on her face. I didn't know what came over me, for the past few days I had been submerged in black short comings that Lisa just happen to be the straw the tipped over the haystack.

"Im, Immm so sorry Lisa I didn't..."

"You did! I mean you think I don't know what I am, you think I like how people treat me taking my kindness as weakness. This whole time I thought you was helping me by letting me vent but hearing what you just said I realized that this was the first time somebody has truly helped me. I don't drive but if I could tag a ride with you when we close I would love to hear Omar speak."

I nodded and we worked in silence for the remainder of the operational day. The darkness had consumed the sky and the cold air confronted us the moment we exited the store. We prepared ourselves for the harsh cold the inside of the car had waiting for us. The cold leather seats felt like ice when our warm bodies sat on them. The cold air blasted our faces as the ignition started the car. I pulled out of the drive way and headed towards the north end.

"I thought we was going to the SG" She asked.

"We are I just have to pick up one of my classmates from school, I invited her as well"

"Is she like me?" she asked with a look of shame.

"Your nothing to look down on Lisa, if it makes you feel any better I just woke up to reality as well. It's the culture that we were brought up in that promotes this redundant type thinking amongst all of us. She is like not just you but all of us in a sense of accepting what is and dismissing her true potential. So no she is not like you, she is like us."

It seemed the comfort in not being alone caused her to crack a smile, I looked at her and smiled back "It's funny how one of the first heart to heart moments we have is talking about how we aint shit!" She said as we both broke down laughing.

We pull up to her house and we both walk up and rung the doorbell. Her mother answered and I know by the look on her face she felt her past had just knocked on her door. Living in the north end of town she clawed her way through college, scraped pennies and became the door mat for her superiors until she was able to open her own practice. In her mind she was doing her daughter a favor for taking her out of the place she had come from and raising her in the higher class area where complexions were frosted.

"Alisha your friends are here to take you away" She yelled up the stairs. I could tell that Alisha had told her mom about where she was going and that her mother had tried to talk her out of it.

"Look I don't care what she says if you are truly her friends then you would not be taking her to Saints Grove and have her ruin everything her and I have worked for. I'm from a place much worse than Saints Grove and hell will freeze over before I let that area disrupt what she has going on!" Her mother protested.

She was just like the people Omar had preached about. The ones that so called made it in life and move away alienating themselves from there people calling themselves educated blacks and the others niggas.

"I assure you ma'am that it is not my intention to see that her education stop in fact it is the exact opposite. We are going to hear a lecture on African American enterprise, entrepreneurship and ways to fight the negative stereotypes that plague our black community. I will be more than happy to leave my contact information and give you the exact address of where we will be located. You can rest well to know that your daughter's safety is always the top priority and understand that I see myself as a true gentleman that makes sure the ladies get back safe. I will be waiting in the car so that you may have any last minute words with your daughter with privacy. Thank you for allowing me time to speak with you."

She looked at me speechless and nodded as Lisa and I headed to the car.

"What the hell was that! You sounded like one of our professors" She said laughing

"Honestly I don't know where that came from"

"well with them words you should put that in a book or something. Lord knows more people need to hear that to wake them the hell up."

Before I could respond I saw Alisha jump down the stairs and run to the car. The way she was running you would think we was going to a club, road trip or something. She opened the door and slid into the backseat.

"I don't know what you said to my mom but she said that I should find a person like you!" When Alisha said that Lisa and I almost died laughing.

The road to the SG seemed like the longest road trip. We filled the car with laughter and jokes about how mean me and Lisa's boss was and how boring me and Alisha's professor was. We spoke of the white customers we had verses the white classmates we learned by. We spoke not of our hatred for them for none existed; we didn't share the turmoil our ancestors did going through it with whites however we did speak of the worries we as a community had that were absent from the white neighborhoods. Alisha spilled her feelings of feeling absent In the black community, feeling cheated that she didn't get to be raised around her people because she wasn't raised in the hood; while Lisa spoke of how she felt disadvantage because she did get raised in the hood and not some privileged location. Although their feelings were real they were miss placed. The hood didn't have to be a source of pain. It could be a gathering of people trying to support each other, low income didn't have to translate into poverty. Low income in unison could collaborate to invest in real estate and own property, families could combine to continue to buy and own property to increase their financial portfolio. Combined efforts could establish businesses that employ members of that community and serve the community they reside in, in response the community would use their buying power at that establishment creating wealth that circulates the community instead of leave. The hood also didn't have to be the black hole Lisa saw it as and Alisha didn't have to view black struggle in the hood as a rite of passage. Negative stereotypes show that in order to be considered black you had to use slang, dress in a certain fashion and act a certain way. How toxin this form of thinking is I thought.

We shared words between us until we arrived at our final destination. The graffiti amplified the closer we got to SG. Alisha seemed like a big-eyed country kid that had her first city view. She thought the gang signs splattered over the business walls were beautiful works of art. We found parking amongst the sea of vehicles. The church was jam packed. When we finally discovered a resting place for the car the ladies and I headed into the holy facility.

"Damn bruh I thought you was married nigga. Who dez ladies?" Jared asked. Jared was One of my old classmates back in high school that simply stayed in high school mentally.

Lisa kept walking right by as if his comment went to deaf ears. Alisha stopped however and seemed shy not making eye contact.

"Naw these ladies are just my friends from work and school." I reluctantly responded guiding Alisha away to an open spot.

I could tell Alisha had never been around a group of black people. It was amazing how out of place a black person could be amongst other blacks. She was excited almost as if she was visiting another country and embracing a culture that she had only read about.

"My mom would freak out if she was here!" She joked.

"No your mom would freak out at how you reacting. You stand out like a white person In here and your beauty makes you a topic of interest to these fellas in here." I said.

"Thank you" she said blushing.

"That's just it, that's why your momma is scared for you because that simple line made you blush. These cats out here got game that can sweep you off your feet if you don't know your true worth. Just know not just here but anywhere, you make them earn your trust through action not mere words. It takes no effort to say something but it can take everything out of you to be what you said." I lectured.

She looked at me as if she was mentally jotting everything I said down. "Yea your right, I guess I haven't heard anyone break it down to me like that before."

Lisa looked back at me and smiled, she gestured with her hand scribbling on her palm that I'm guessing was a pad and mouthed write a book. I rolled my eyes and looked onward to the podium.

At once the room started clapping and cheering, I drew my attention toward the direction of the praises and saw Omar in front of the podium. His black gown seemed to tailor his slim tall figure. His head was freshly shaved and it seemed to have a wax polish on it as it reflected the light that bounced off his head. He was the most powerful person on the planet to me at that moment. He raised both his hands with his fingers opened toward the crowd to silence the wave of people.

With his usual thunderous voice he says

WAKE UP!!!!!!

Chapter 22

2 Tone

I take the last swig of Hennessey out the bottle and head out the door. Scoobie and Jess chauffeur me to link up with Ross. Out of all my weeks this year this week had to be the worst. The betrayal of Rome sat heavy on my mind and Ross poor performance couldn't have come at a worst time. Bones death also flooded my mind, never once had I regretted busting shots but Bone's bullet maybe should had stayed in the chamber. I was also rethinking the whole drive by shooting towards Ali. I had little to no intel besides what Ross had given me. I was always known for doing my research and making strategic moves but I blasted at Ali off the strength of a crooked ass cops word. I didn't trust Ross but he was a necessary evil in order to business.

My ego I have to admit had cause the blunt of the pain I endured this week. My ambition to control everything and not monitor all my affairs had me bite off more than I bargained for. An all-out war was sparking out between me and them South Tacoma boys and I didn't even have the unity of my own crew. The police pressure also leaked into my life bring a lot of attention halting my business.

I show a face of confidence though. My followers can't know that I made such mistakes. I created an enemy taking out Ali's daughter and the only way to clean that slat was with his blood. As long as there is breath in his body I know he would breathe revenge and keep seeking me out. Without Rome in my corner I felt lonely. He was really the only one I fully trusted and now he was doing the will of another.

My anger still was high on the topic of Rome making me reminisce on Lashandria's body. If Rome ever truly found out he would probably team up with Ali in hunting me down. Lashandria was a liability I had created and Rome may have to be dealt with if it ever came to that. Too much blood shed would defiantly lead to me creating more attention towards myself. I felt like the walls were closing in on me so I took the blunt to the face to get me some room.

Hennessey and weed always gave me a sort of invincible not caring feeling. I loved it and I knew I would need to be at a certain mind set to hear what the hell Ross was going to tell me. Good news never seemed to flow from his mouth these days. I ignore the weird feeling of okaying the meet up around the church. Why the fuck would he want to meet there?

"Yo bruh its packed as hell. Is there an event going on or something here?" Scoobie said interrupting my thoughts.

"Shit I don't know, but I aint feelin this shit. Let me hit this mouthafucka up." I said dialing Ross.

Cordell

My pocket vibrates as I chase down a beer after a shot of vodka. The beer is flat and warming up from me paying no attention as I watched the game. I had just left the office ready for the festivities that was going to take place. I feel for my phone in my pocket and pull it out to see Tone.

"Tone my man what's shaking."

"What's shaking my ass why the hell you pick this hot ass spot to have a meet up. I aint feeling this shit. Where you at?" he suspiciously question.

"Im almost there, relax were not going to exchange a brick of cocaine or nothing." I said laughing.

"Yea whatever just get here or I'm checking out."

"Don't worry I will be there in a jiff just be across the street in the Alley." I reassured.

I shifted from Tone and pressed Ali in the contact.

Ali

"Hello, Man where the fuck is he! I been posted up for a minute waiting on your call!"

Ross finally came through for once as he gave me Tone's exact coordinates.

"Let's get this nigga, shoot over there to the alley." I instructed Isaiah.

Isaiah was a young nigga eager to prove himself. He wouldn't hesitate to bust shots and took anybody not respecting his territory as a personal insult. He was reckless but this was a reckless mission so he fit the puzzle.

Roman

I'm running late smashing down I-5, I had to pick up Lashandria from work. I know the words are already pouring from Omar's mouth so I take every yellow light as a green one trying to get there. I hurry not only because I'm late but also because I know Lashandria senses the attitude I'm giving off. Her laying with my best friend is starting to weigh on me. My new found moral code is preventing me from acting out like I would have done had I found out a few days earlier.

Lashandria

The distance between us is undeniable in this small car speeding to the church. I don't understand what has gotten him this way. I try to make small talk but he closes my attempts with a shorter response. Omar usually makes him more open so maybe after we get out of the gathering he will be more open to tell me what's wrong. At the same time my mind keeps convincing me that it's not my secret that he is mad about. It must be something else, anything else for that matter. Anything is better than him being mad at me for my none loyal actions.

Shivers run through my body when I see Tones car in the alley as we pulled up to the packed church looking for a parking space. I hadn't seen Tone since our last interaction and I defiantly didn't want to see him now.

Ali

"There that bitch nigga is pull up Isaiah!" I said pointing at the ally at his deem lite Monte Carlo.

Isaiah wiped hard in the alley turning on the high beams to blind the passengers.

Roman

What the hell? Why is Tone in the alley and who is that riding up on him? O shit!

"Babe stay here if you hear any shots you take off and go home!" I yelled

"No baby, please stay here with me, Please!!!" her pleas become more faint the closer I sprint to the alley. I was running towards Andre not Tone, I knew he was still in there somewhere. Tone had defiled my woman, troubled this community and through his leadership my family was put in danger but Andre was still in there confused and just trying to survive the only way he knew how.

Chapter 23

Omar

Wake up Black Students!

"All too many times the keys to freedom have been trapped in between the pages of books. The black community continually falls behind in the academic arena compared to other races. Black students are not associated with high SAT or ACT scores, high state exam testing or being a member of the high GPA percentile of their class. At the same time, black students are regarded as highly talented athletes. This is only a repeat cycle of the world respecting our physical traits instead of our mental capacity. That black student may be a marvelous running back but he will never own the team. Most of the time the owner of the team never even played a day on the field. What does this tell us? If you ask me the message is that we don't own our talent! Need more proof prepare yourself for the next section.

The 3-top professional athletic institutions, NFL, NBA and MLB together house 92 teams most of them having many black and Latino star athletes and yet we only own 2 percent of the NBA, 0 percent in the NFL and MLB domain. However, we are 74 percent of the NBA, over 60 percent of the NFL and 8 percent of the MLB with Latinos being 28 percent together making 36 percent of the MLB with no ownership. The NBA's 30 teams net worth is 5.2 billion, NFL top 10 teams are worth 66 billion with the average teams being worth about 2.3 billion, The MLB is worth 36 billion! A lot of money that we hand an extraordinary hand in building and yet we own practically nothing! We celebrate athletics in our community and have no idea about the low-test scores of our black youth. Many people know Nike and Adidas stars that strike record breaking sales but don't know the owners Phil Knight and Adolf Dassler. Well at least we own the music industry, right? Sony BMG CEO Doug Morris, Universal Music Group CEO Lucian Charles Grainge, Warner Music Group CEO Stephen F. Cooper own over 80 percent of the music industry! These are just the big 3! What do we truly own. How about government, 535 seats in the senate and representatives and we hold 43 seats, Latinos hold 32 seats and Asians 30. Together we represent 19.6 percent of congress while the white holds just above 80 percent. More specifically blacks are 8 percent of congress. It's everywhere, look at the car you drive, who is the CEO of that? The company that makes your everyday household items. There are only 5 CEOs out of the 500 major companies that look like you and I. That's 1 percent people! In 1994, there were 54 African American owned banks per the FDIC now there are 21. There are 6900 banks in America and we own less than 1 percent. We can go on and on and make this book thicker than the bible of what we do not own. Wake up!

Knowledge is the vaccination that prevents the social inequality disease. Education is medicine that fights and protects you from multiple societal diseases, however to keep the medicine effective it needs to be taken continuously. As with traditional remedies; germs, bacteria and disease evolve to survive the dosage eventually rendering the drug ineffective. To combat this problem, we must up the dosage. Knowledge works the same way with society. The world around us is continuously changing and we must adapt to these changes with new learning. In general, the black community shot record isn't up to date. We are behind on our vaccinations and we continually become ill with low income, dead end employment, promotion barriers, and social alienation. We use school to find steady employment as aspirin which only relives the pain of complying bills just making the bare minimum payments. Even with this according to the government 69 percent of blacks graduate high school in 2011-2012 and they reported that as an all-time high! So, I guess a D plus is good for us. We are showing progress with a 72 percent graduation rate, C minus. We are A plus people that are sleeping in class lets wake up because true knowledge allows us to find ways to establish financial independence which is the cure."

I see Lisa and Alisha's eyes glued to Omar hanging on to his every word. I can tell that his words are working on them.

"Ask a child what he or she desires to be in the future and 9 times out of 10 its to work for somebody. I want to be a police officer, firefighter, solider, lawyer, doctor, dentist. Children usually don't say own my own practice, start my own law firm, start my own security company! Children only think of finding traditional "I work for you" employment instead of creating a business and or organization that creates employment for many and impacts many more.

High school students need more than just the traditional curriculum of math, humanities, and English. They need financial budgeting, accounting, credit education, Real estate, and economics. We have none of these courses offered and yet the credit card companies feel you know enough about credit when they send you a card in the mail *when you turn 18. The current high school syllabus teaches our youth how to follow already crowded paths. The syllabus I desire for our youth is the one that teaches them how to clear a path making a way for others to follow. Standard educational systems breed managers where knowledge of the market and asset building breeds leaders. Schools, especially in the black and Latino community need to teach entrepreneurship, tax education, accounting, economics and marketing courses as part of their curriculum. These are the courses that lays the foundation of building a business. The reason why blacks are so far behind is because our schools invest in stadiums and theaters instead of these courses. The school system is falling behind with the ever-changing world around us. Waiting on the schools to pass an educational proposal has a lengthy time-period, we need this knowledge now! Parents and students need to search for this information which is at a click of a button. There are mountains of financial, business ownership, marketing, and small business books all over. We can self-educate our-selves on these topics if we so choose to look at our resources. I firmly believe that once the mass is awoken mountains will become pebbles, oceans puddles, and the sky too low of a ceiling. The true potential will turn into fully explored energy that forces reality to transform into fantasy."*

The crowd hung on to every word the dripped from Omar's mouth. I was able to tell who was a first timer to hear Omar speak because of their reactions. The shock of surprise of someone hearing the cold raw truth. The audience generated a huge source of Amen and preach on as they usually did. He continued.

"It can't stop at just the money though. You see that isn't our only problem and not even the worst if you ask me. The worst problem we have is nigga! Nigga is nigger! A hateful, spiteful word. A word meant to dehumanize us has been transformed to a word we us for our brother and best friend. A word that we use for a loyal companion. So, I guess we can surpass a word dipped in our ancestor's blood and dignity and own it but can't own our position in society! Hey I need to take time out of this speech to give credit to the person that was right and when your right your right so I must acknowledge the winner of this round. Jim Crow was right! He can contain the African American people. Stripping us off our original names, our land, customs, and traditions. You think oppression is over! You think segregation is over. Look in your house of representatives, look at your congress, look and your supreme court justice officials, look at your fortune 500 companies, look at your CEOs, look at your high-ranking military command, Look at your governors, police Chiefs etc. Now turn to another section and look at your criminal justice system, looks pretty separated to me. You see a few sprinkles sure, but you tell me are you satisfied with that. Do you think we have made it! Let me rewind this and take you back in time.

Children stripped away from their parent's, husband separated from their wives. Our ancestor's bodies were deemed products to be bought and sold at discretion of masters, our blood was worth no more than the currency used to purchase our ancestors, and their potential was only measured by their labor to produce output for their owners. That's our history! History's Hatred took many of our ancestors through lynching's, and other torturous deaths.

That is our history! Oppression through segregation, alienation, Degradation created huge barriers for our people. That is our history! Police brutality, unjust laws, unfair practices prevented progress in our ancestors walk through life. That is our history! Our ancestors gathering havens were burned, bombed, shot up and demolished. That was our history!

You see when we only view the darkness in our past we become blind to our triumphs, our courage, our determination, and our future. We have been victims for far too long and we must open our eyes to see that in these days and times we are our own oppressors. We see the world as a trap instead of an opportunity. We feel our stereotypes is in grained in our DNA and thus cannot be changed! We embrace being late calling it CP time, we embrace our women as expendable calling ourselves players, we embrace our ignorance calling ourselves my nigga! We don't allow other racist to call us nigga....no that's disrespectful right, we feel only we should disrespect ourselves and call ourselves nigga. We have embraced a culture that our ancestors tried to crawl out off. We reject our community and don't invest in our land while our ancestors were slaves to it. We voluntarily part from our families while our ancestors were stolen from theirs. The biggest difference between the African Americans past and its present is that the past was forced into submission while the present allows submission."

All the pain was placed on our minds when he was speaking. The nightmare had to be so horrific in order to wake us up. Tears began to pour from some member's face in the audience. Omar kept up the heat letting it all out as he continued with his words.

I do want to say we have some superstars among us. We have had individuals break through numerous barriers. I'm proud of the pioneers who conquered a victory. I am so honored to be a part of the African American legends of the civil rights movement, the military, the scholars, the athletes, the entertainers etc. We have come a long way! This section is not intended to start a race war it is intended to put perspective in our history so that we may grind in the present to enjoy further accomplishments in the future. Our past legends have only implemented stage one, which was to gain human rights and show the world that we can compete. Okay point proven, our warriors can jump, run, read, write, discover, invent and fight with the best of them. You see we as a people tend to ride the wave of a few. We quickly shout out Mohammad Ali, Michael Jordan, James Brown, Oprah, Jackie Robinson, Lebron James, MLK, Malcolm X, Obama and the list goes on. We sing these names loud and proud and yet your own name doesn't go far. We Idolize the work of the few and then we ourselves just do average work if that. We quote words of prominent African American figures and yet your own words most of the time mean nothing. Actions of the past seem to be diluted to stories, stories meant to entertain instead of lessons meant to teach the mass how to strive as they have done. You see it is not nor has it ever been just enough for Obama to be the first black president. That's a battle won in a losing war. You see to win the war political science classes, law classrooms and candidate selections for government offices need to be flooded with black participates.

Government job openings need to be consumed by black applications. The police, fire and EMS academies need to go through countless black applications before we call ourselves making true progress. These powerful black leaders are examples on how to pass a test, and in order to pass we must all participate. White people don't feel pride when another white man takes office, there not surprised when their CEO is white, and that is because they expect success within their people. Now on the flip side a Black General in the Army everyone wants to celebrate, or a black CEO we feel times has changed, but why is that a surprise? Why are we shocked when blacks climb through the ranks or when a black person is the first to do something, but we are not shocked when police pull us over unjust, or when the prison system is filled with blacks or when you see a black lady mopping floors at a hotel. The answer is we expect eating crumbs off the floor and are blown away when we see a black person eating at the table.

I have always known that we were able to run a country that's why I was never shocked when Obama won the race. I have always known that we could reach billionaire status that's why I wasn't surprised when Oprah joined the ranks of the other billionaires. I expect success amongst my people. What has blown me away is that the African American community still stays asleep after all the nightmares history has given us. We have still yet as a people woken up to the potential of our own hands and the opportunity we have to build something.

You see black power isn't just 28 days sometimes 29 if it resides in leap year in February. Black power is a way of life, the way you carry yourself, the way you treat your neighbor all year round, your ability to build an asset, and your ability to be not just a productive member in society, your household and your children's lives but a flourishing member.

Now let's awaken the army! Let the mass show the world that we can impact America even further! Our legends are single cells in the body but the black community is the sum of all its parts. Thugs, gangsters and OG's stop justifying making your property value go down with illegal activities. Incarcerated brothers free yourself through knowledge and come out productive citizens. Military brothers rise through the ranks. Black business owners flourish in your markets. Consumers indulge in what your brothers and sisters have to offer. Entertainers feed the media not only the truth of your burden past and sinful ways because the truth is the truth and it surely needs to be heard but also show light to the all the good. Brothers and sisters stop hating on one another and start appreciating. Sisters show class and brothers show professionalism. Impeach the pimps, and gangsters and vote in the real heroes. Join hands with the other races in America that are celebrating in their successes. The black communities need to have a seat at the table with the rest of them, not just serving them.

Black communities don't like what the media says about us, let us be our own reporters then. We feel the government doesn't represent us, vote, run for office and fund our own campaigns. Don't agree with law enforcement tactics, join the force and diversify the blue shield. Single mother working two jobs and cannot monitor her children let the community step in and guide the young children and the list goes on! We can change anything we want to thanks to the sacrifice off the ones before us. College is expensive but many books are cheap and the internet is free. Martin Luther King taught us how to march, Malcom X taught us to defend ourselves, Harriet Tubman taught us to leave no one behind, Fredrick Douglas taught us to preserver and the Tuskegee airman taught us to fly. Use these lessons! Build from your father's mistakes and your mother's bad decisions and capitalize on their strengths. Use your obstacles as motivations, and your failures as second chances. I know it takes time to change, but since we are talking about change I feel it's about that time. Freedom is right there! I know we have been set free from many things but the finish line is still just up ahead. Gather brothers and sisters gather!! I pray that these words are flowing through your body! Let the adrenalin spark your desires, let the adrenalin put fire to your ambition, and let the adrenalin ignite your power!! It's always been there but I feel our environment has finally brought it out of us! Its fight or flight time people and I said once so here it is again, the flights have all been cancelled! Rise and kick the blankets of self-oppression off you, lift your head off that comfortable pillow of justification, Get out of the victimization mattress! Stand up on the ground of your community, open the curtains of ownership and look at your market!!! Jim Crow its round two now and let's see if fighting a sleeping man is the same as fighting an alert one! I think we are up now!"

The crowd had a deafening roar of praise! Hands clapping sounded like a full stampede of hooves colliding into the ground. The energy of religion seem to collaborate with the focus of unity and ownership. I look over at Alisha and Lisa and saw the spirit flow through them as they parade and rejoice with the rest of them. Omar was electrifying, rally the people up.

The parking lot and streets were flooded after his speech as though the last day of school had let out. Although the crowd was thick with people I still found it strange that I hadn't seen Roman. I had seen Jeff, Tyson and Roger over at the far end of the parking lot and noticed that many people I knew to be a part of the shadow business had also attended. The crowd was diverse with people from all walks of life within the same community.

We waited until the crowd reduced in size when I could introduce them to Omar. We walked back into the alter were Omar was talking with the Islamic lady." asalamalakim brother Darrius," walaikum salam I replied as we approached them. Lisa and Alisha eyes swelled with admiration when they I introduced them to Omar. He was humbled by their compliments to his speaking.

"thank you, ladies I am really happy to be your servant of inspirational words, If I could please trouble you for a moment with Darrius I will return him to you." Omar requested. They pleasantly allowed his request as we took a few steps down the walk way.

"You have to be ready for the hurt Darrius, this whole time I have shown you the presence of god despite what may appear to be hell on earth. He has always and forever will be with you. Now you must be the rebuilder and restorer."

"What do you mean, your building a whole army of followers that chant your name the moment you appear to speak."

"No I destroyed their old way of thinking, I wrecked their existence to the truth of prosperity if they so choose to go that route. The old way of thinking made it easy to accept this situation however you are charged with rebuilding and restoring a better platform from the old platform I destroyed. You must follow me swiftly for even though I knocked the old house down weeds will grow in its place if you do not reestablish its foundation."

"I haven't been the one speaking and moving the crowd you have, you talk as though your leaving tomorrow."

"I am leaving but I will be back in a few days to check on you, also understand this that death doesn't mean the end. Many times, the death of one can give life to many. The lessons I have taught still apply despite any hardship that the future brings."

Omar words seem to be random without proper transitions. He went from being ready for death and it not being the end. I nodded at his words not understanding his point and decided to be the one to disappear, I signaled the girls to head out. Out of now where it seemed the blast of guns filled the air! Like wind blowing a pile of leaves people where everywhere trying to escape the danger zone.

I raced over to the car and hurried the ladies in, I still didn't see Romen and decided to chauffeur the girls home and hit Rome up on the way back.

Chapter 24

Tone

The white light is blinding but I can still make out two people coming quick for me. I know what this is and immediately know why Ross planned the meet up here. I throw my whole body down beneath the dash board. I see Scoobie at the corner of my eye reach for his heat but the car is to cramp to move the weapon out in time. They blast at my car glass going everywhere and the bullets ripping my car apart.

Fuck this can't be how this shit end! They stop blasten and I know they are moving closer to the car to finish the job. I take the suspended fire to reach for Scoobie side piece and pop up blasting through the windshield making him dance to the bullets. I empty the whole clip making every bullet count, hitting his body!

Ali

I dodge the returned fire behind my passenger door and hear Isaiah fall to the ground.

"Isaiah! Fuck!" I yelled. All he ever wanted to do was prove himself and because of my war path he paid the ultimate price. I could hear my heart pounding and my blood seem to be heating up my whole body! At this point Tone has taken far too many of my people! I drop the half empty clip and loaded a fresh one. Tone was going to pay for this shit! I rise and point my barrel right at the passenger door seeing Tone trying to pull for his other gun. I beat him to it though, my eyes meet his and I know he knows he lost this draw. My finger begins to squeeze on the trigger before a hard object smashes my head from behind.

Roman

I don't think I just act. I know Ali could turn around at any moment to take me out but he doesn't. He's too fixed on Tone. I see a piece of side walk free from the curb and reach down scooping up the rock and make it just in time before he could pull the trigger. Blood sprays the surrounding areas from the impact. He humps over the door dropping his Glock.

Tone

"Hell yea nigga and here I thought you didn't care about a nigga anymore!"

I hear the commotion of scattering in the streets, the screeching tires on the pavement fleeing the scene, and the screams of people calling upon others to "get out of the way" and "come on." I look over to the driver of my car and see Scoobie's lifeless body. The assault happened so quick he barely had time to respond. The blood decorated the inside of my vehicle and the anger swelled up inside me.

I look over to Ali struggling to regain conciseness and his composer. The gash on the back of his head had him leaking all over the alley street. Roman had saved my life but instead of feeling grateful for my life I felt revenge to take Ali's. I finish loading my piece and loaded the bullet in the chamber. Ali sees me coming the way I want him to. I want him to feel his time is limited; I want him to know I will be his Grim Reaper. He crawls away as I kick his body over. The blow to the gut sends his body into a coughing frenzy. I know the sirens are going to be on their way but I burn my precious get away time for the execution I was about to commit. I stand over his body and point the heat right at his face.

"Tone! No, I didn't save your life for this! Let's go, it's time to go! You don't have to continue this spare his life and let's go!" Roman cried out

"Naw my nigga, Im indebted to you sure enough but this man has a debt to be paid with Scoobies life and with him trying to take mine that must be paid!"

"Bruh, look this shit has got to stop we can't be this way anymore! Tone give me the gun."

Ali

I see his eyes and know there is no freewill in him. He is a slave to his hatred and saw myself standing over me with the gun. No doubt this is how I wanted the situation to end but with me standing over him. His mind is already made up so I don't waste my last seconds pleading. That's what he wants and I will not give him the satisfaction.

I know I won't see my daughter again in heaven because the hate I had and what I was going to do isn't going to grant me entry into those golden gates. I brought flames to my whole community for years spreading drugs and anarchy to the hood so it's only fitting that I will probably see Tone in hell. I hear Roman beg on my behalf but I cut him off.

"Fuck you nigga! I will see yo bitch ass in hell!" My final words rang out.

Roman

Blood sprays on my shoes from the gun blast as I tried to reach for Tone to give me the gun.

"Noooooo! Fuck noooooo! What the hell is this!" I yelled.

"What the hell you mean nigga! Ima let this nigga come back for me and othas in my fam! Nigga you think he would had hesitated to pull the strap on you if he would had saw you coming! Nigga if wanted this sucka nigga to live then you should had let this nigga pull the trigga! Look we got to go nigga come on!" Tone said

I didn't want to take another step in his direction but my body still moved towards the passenger seat. I was on auto pilot as we rode away from the crime scene. The smell of sweet metal consumed the air as the ground had begun to take on fresh rain. The night felt so still in the heat filled environment in the car.

"Nigga I had my doubts and all but bro if you want out I got you. My life was supposed to be gone my nigga and since you gave me a second chance you got yours, clean slate with me. You free out these streets homie." Tone said. His twisted view of a second chance brought sickness to my gut. The man that grants second chances was the same one who took a life out of this world. His tormented demeanor brought even more depression when I realized I had rescued a killer. Andre was no more in that body. The cancer had completely engulfed his body and he would infect the whole community if he wasn't cut out. The worst part about it was the fact that up until a few days ago I saw eye to eye with this man. I couldn't hold my breath any longer. The rain began to fall more rapidly. I had wondered if this rain was for cleansing the block or watering the infestation.

"No Andre! We done! Not me but you too, I can't let you keep burying all of us! U just put a bullet through his head like it wasn't shit! You so disconnected wit life that you think it's nothing to kill somebody! This business we in is filling up body bags and putting people in the dirt and you just on somewhat ever shit! You can't deal wit the consequences of your actions so you just kill off the source! I'm done fuckin with you Andre and Im endin this shit!"

"What you mean you endin this shit! Nigga this aint no book you get done reading and you just shelf me! Nigga this is life and niggas knew the rules when they signed up so all this sympathy for the dead is hypocritical. That nigga would have taken any life I would have and you feelin sorry for that nigga!"

"Nigga sign up! Did that little girl signed up when she got hit! Did my daughter and lady sign up when my house got shot up!"

"Man fuck yo lady! I tell you what she wasn't saying shit when you was funding her before she had yo daughter! When times got rough she dissed you and you feeling sorry for a bitch that hoped on this dick before she confided in her man so fuck her! Fuck that girl and..."

I take control over the steering wheel and we swerve right into an open alley and smash right into the dumpsters. My head collides with the windshield as we both settled in our seats after the collision.

Tone

100 bells is going of in my head as I open my eyes to my cloudy sight. The taste of blood fills my mouth. I look over at Roman finding the strength to get out the car, it seemed like he teleported to my side as I felt the door open and he pulls me out the car. Sharp pain pieces the side of my face as his fist nearly dismantles my jaw! I fall to the ground rolling over spitting out blood. My pain sensors sound off again when his foot goes through my stomach! I can't tell if it's the rain or the blood that has me soaking wet but my mouth gets more blood as his knuckles go head to head with my teeth.

Chapter 25

Darrius

It seemed like somebody had stretched the road as the ride seemed long to just be going around the corner to where Lisa resided. The theatrics of the night was enough to keep us all entertained in our thoughts. We each let the scenery pass as we reflected on the word that brought freedom to the actions that brought death. No one knew where the shots came from or why. Like roaches we scattered stepping on one another, pushing each other and literally responding the way Omar told us not to. None of us went back for others left behind everyone grabbed their own and let the others fend for themselves. The fear of death has the hardest test to pass when it's quizzing you on your compassion for others.

Lisa like me was used to the turmoil that the hood brings. The shootings let us know we are home while the bullet rings let Alisha know she is a long way from her comfort zone. Alisha was shaking her leg, probably one of her coping mechanisms.

"My mom was right. I always thought that she was trying to control every little thing that I do but instead I realize that she was trying to protect me. How could someone just open fire like that with all those people around. I will never understand why there is so much violence even at a peaceful rally; and black folks wonder why they are always policed and monitored! It's because they act like animals!" Alisha cried out.

"They? Did you just say they? You say they as though you don't share the same heritage! You say they as though we are not attached to you! Let me tell you something it's easy to see opportunity when you are flying high in the sky and can see all your avenues but most people here are at ground level deep in the forest and can barely see the next time they will eat or how they will pay rent to keep a roof over their head! People at the top of the food chain will never understand the prey that just tries to survive. When you go home you tell your mom about the unity we had. About the work we need to do to get to a community like the one you was born into. She needs to hear news of change not the same old news she is used to hearing. Channel 5 will do that for her in the morning. This shit happens all the time here and babies grow up in this mess that creates scared men. The people out here have so much fear for one another that they will shoot them dead before they try and make peace. And white people only approach us with a side arm holstered to their belt. I'm tired of this madness and I want you to use this to fuel you to promote good instead of letting fear keep you away from your kind. Know this also no matter how many white friends you surround yourself with at the end of the day when a stranger see you they see the same stereotypes the see us all in." Lisa defended.

The first time I heard Lisa speak up was not for herself but for her people. Alisha's silence let me know that she was soaking in Lisa's words while Lisa's outburst let me know she was looking at this life with knew glasses seeing things for how they really are. Silence consumed the car once again when we pulled up into Lisa's apartment complex.

"I will see you tomorrow?" Lisa said

I nodded and began the ride to the Northside which seemed like a really quick ride compared to the short car ride down a few blocks to Lisa's as we pulled up to Alisha's house.

"You must think I'm scary and weak?" Alisha said as we pulled up to her drive way.

"No, I think that you just realized how weak our people have become. Only the strong build dynasties and massive empires while the weak merely tries to establish themselves in the stronger's world. Your fear is not a weakness, it's a sign that somethings wrong. Your strength is when you try and correct that wrong."

She doesn't say anything after I said that. We sit in the car for a minute and I can tell she is collecting her thoughts. She looks back at me smiling saying.

"The next time another rally comes up let me know so I can be there." With that request, she left the car walking up to her house where the living room lights greeted her, probably from her mom still waiting up for her daughter.

As I pull off from her house heading back towards Saints grove I try to call Rome. His phone had been kicking me to voice mail for a minute and I didn't see him at the rally. I knew he could probably give me some insight on who was doing the shooting. The phone follows the habit of the voice mail as I arrive back in SG.

The blue and red lights occupy the streets as officer's man hunt for the shooters are in progress, I tried to drive past the church but was rerouted when police barricaded one block. I could see the ambulance inside the cordoned area and what seemed to be a detective speaking with a uniformed officer. I turned right to bypass the police assembly. Seeing the ambulance made me realize a bullet probably found a home in someone. As I turn the detective eyes made contact with mine as I drove past.

Stone

I don't know why the driver catches my attention but I watch as he turns down the street and follow his tail lights until it vanishes to the next block. The officer informs me on his initial scene evaluation and I prepare myself for what lies beyond the yellow tape. I immediately draw my attention to a young man no more than 19 lying lifeless on the ground. Even though the rain was coming down the pool of blood around his corpse was still bright red. The gun still rest in his hands and right away I know he had the same intentions his killer had. I walk beyond the young man and see another black man riddled with bullets. His blood contaminated the whole interior of the car, there are bullet casing scattered around the whole area. I recognize the car and know I have my first suspect, Andre. Things where definitely heating up in the streets because Andre knew we were watching his every move and yet he allowed himself to be vulnerable in an area with many witnesses. His career criminal resume was lengthy to say the least but this work was sloppy and not the MO of his discreet actions.

I hear one of the officers scream medic and run to his location to find my third victim coughing up blood. It was Ali! The father of the little girl who had been shot. Judging by the position of the first victim I knew they were together on this one and sought revenge for Andre! He has to make it I told myself, medics seem to have taken every piece of their equipment off the truck to stabilize Ali, shooting Oxygen in his body and applying pressure to all leaking areas. The medics load his body on the stretcher while the other two get packaged in body bags. I dial Cordell so many times that his number filled my call log and still he had no answer. The medics did a rapid transport to the hospital as I stayed behind helping officers gather evidence. The crowd around the scene had grew and for the first time I was called over to speak with them.

Witnesses threw more information than I could write and the participation to find justice was over whelming! They look as though they were tired, and sick of the constant violence. My presence usually caused alienation from the community but now they all had an inviting tone. I knew my case was solved before I left the crime scene, the community had finally started to see the thugs for who they really were and for once in my whole criminal justice career I had seen eye to eye with the people I was sworn to protect. I launch my car towards the hospital speeding the whole way to ensure my number one witness stays alive.

Lashandria

I don't know where he is! I don't even know what fully happened! I beat my hand on the steering wheel hitting every structure in the car screaming! The tears from my eyes to the rain drops on the windshield makes me feel like I am looking underwater. It's so hot in the car that I roll down my window to the chill of the night allowing rain to sprinkle in. I can't seem to catch my breath, and my heart can't get a steady rhythm. I raise my hands to wipe the tears from my eyes while the cool breeze chills my body blowing on the sweat my underarms had produced.

I just couldn't believe it. The man I love saved the man I defiled myself with, the guilt of his destiny is mine fully because I should have told him! I should had stopped him when he ran for Tone's rescue. My selfish reason to hold my own secret to avoid the consequences now has played out in the worst scenario.

I didn't even know where to start looking. I must see him before the cops catch up to him, Why, why did I let this happen. When he told me to stay in the car I did it with no rebuttal and I didn't even attempt to pull him back. I grow tired of hearing the dial tone, all my calls have gone straight to voicemail and my texts have gone unanswered. I need help because I can't do this! I need to find him. All my contacts seem useless in my phone but I find one number that will help me.

Chapter 26

Darrius

The whole scenery can fit in the palm of my hand as I press my hands against the small window. Trees look like blades of grass and huge bodies of water appear as puddles at this height. The land looks like patches sown together to make a blanket covering the earth. The clouds blind my view and I turn away from the window. I laid my head back on my seat, the seat is so comfortable that my body melts into the upholstery. The roaring of the engines seems like a quite purr in my ear. I look into the front of my seat and see a traveler's magazine. I grasp the book and flip through it, my eyes bouncing from page to page from destination to destination. The words do the locations no justice as they attempt to capture the places in a sentence. On this plane, I have seen them all and the letters don't come close to representing the true experiences of the places. I shove the magazine back in the seat in front of me and smile at my progression. Those picture books use to amaze me but now they were unsatisfying. I look around and see my wife, children, brothers, mother, father, friends, Mr. Taylor, Lisa, Alisha, and many other people of my community on the same flight. We all are here traveling together, I felt a true since of accomplishment. I stand out of my seat and Lashandria immediately catches my eye. She sits all alone looking out of the window and doesn't share the smiles of everyone else on the flight.

"Where is Roman I asked her"

She looks at me and the plane begins to shake vibrating my whole body. The turbulence shakes me to the sound of my phone ringing in my pocket and loud banging at my front door.

I wipe the sleep from my eyes, peel my body off the leather couch and reach into my pocket to answer the phone and walk over to the door.

Darrius!!!! Darrius, Im outside open up the damn door!!! Her voice consumes the silence waking me up out of my sleep on my phone as I walk to the door. I twist the bolt back, unravel the chain and open the door. LaShandria was standing there with not a dry spot on her face due to the sweat and tears that masked her. Her chess was rising as if she was trying to consume all the oxygen for herself.

"What's up Lashandria why you screaming." Trying to calm her down.

"He went out with 2 Tone, I told him not to ride out but he wouldn't listen!"

"Why was he with 2 Tone anyway?."

"He wasn't but then he said he was going to help him, he got out the car and told me to stay. He ran over there and they started shooting and I don't know Darrius I just need your help to find him!" She screamed.

Just as she said that my heart stopped beating. A real cold chill creeped up my spine, and my arm was crowded with goosebumps. The warmth of Lashandria's hand woke me out of my daze. Her eyes blood shot her face soaked with tears. I could feel her hands tremble with fear. She was breathing to the point of hyperventilation.

"Lashandria where is he?"

"He went down Pacific and that's all I know, I saw them drive off in somebody else's car!"

We dove in the car and I threw my car keys in the ignition. We raced through the streets seeming to catch every red light on the strip. The night was still, not a leaf seem to move. The dark clouds formed a roof between earth and the sky blocking out the star light. The rain came down pouring with the thick clouds gathering above. The road seems to stretch for miles traveling only 10 Mins up the street. We was just to the freeway before we heard a sound I will never forget.

BANG, BANG, BANG, BANG!!! The shots echoed in the streets.

I slammed the breaks, my head meeting the steering wheel and Lashandria's the dash board. The impact blurred my vision, I could see Lashandria soothing her head with her hands.

"Lashandra are you good?" I inquired

"I'm fine." Right when she answered we both froze for a moment. The location the blast came from last was the next sharp right. I punched the gas and whipped into the alley way. My car pointed right at Roman lying on the ground!

"Roman!!!!!!!" she cried.

"Somebody call an ambulance!" I screamed as We both got out of the car and sprinted to his body. Roman was struggling with life trying to fight death from claiming his soul. He was breathing as if he had just sprinted a mile gasping for any available air. He was bathed in his own blood, the puddle around him spreading its area.

"I toold yyyy yyooouuuu I wassss done." He struggled speaking in between breathing and fluid running down his throat.

"Sssshhhhh. We know baby we know, you are going to make it just hang on." She hopefully preyed.

I looked over towards my car, the lights still shining the spot light on us. The lights reminded me of the dream I had a few nights ago and realized I was dreaming about the future. Could I had really seen this coming? I had known Roman was playing with fire converting all the street members away from the shadow business but I never thought in a million years this would happen.

Sirens in the distant finally came to us. The rotating lights dancing in the night. Our care was immediately replaced with the EMT's loading Roman on the stretcher into the ambulance.

Tears flood my eyes with each key stroke that tells this story from the beginning back to the beginning as the sirens brakes the silent of the night while the rotator lights echoed of the walls of the buildings. The road bowed down to the speeding truck allowing even red lights to be treated as green. Inside the truck time seem to move slowly. I was inches away from the medic but his words rang faint.

"300 joules ready!"

"Ready"

"Clear body"

"Clear!"

His cheat rises with the potential to hit the roof of the ambulance had restraints not been in place. White gauze turns into red sponges as it rest on the entrance and exit wounds. The oxygen masks appear to almost be suffocating him. Hands pound on his chest cracking bones forcing life in his body.

"Stop compressions!'

"Analyzing rhythm, analyzing rhythm." the machine repeatedly says.

"Shock able rhythm detected."

Clear body!"

"Clear!"

His chest bursts up once again.

The medic gets on the radio with the hospital. This is unit 137; I have one black male 27 years old gunshot to the abdomen, shoulder and upper chest right under the left clavicle. Pulse is faint, blood pressure is dropping. Excessive hemorrhaging. IV is already started, epinephrine already administered, shocked twice, continuing CPR. About 10 mike out how copy"

"I copy last, preparing for arrival in 10 mike how copy."

"Copy"

We were speeding from the patients and I's home. Family and friends didn't have what he needed and the cold fact was they were the cause of his suffering. I wasn't optimistic about his recovery; I wasn't hopeful that he would pull through. I instead preyed that the lord forgives his ways and forgive my people. Death where I come from is not the beginning of a new state of existence, it's the stage of judgment where actions will be accounted for. Hs debt would soon be reconciled with the lord that night as his final breath was taken with an agonal gasp.

Our path was blocked as the doctors took over the care from the EMT's. I couldn't wait in the waiting room! Lashandria came in right after me even more distrait than before. I took the keys from her, I stepped out the hospital and pushed my car to the limit heading back to the SG. He knew, he had always known! All the things I thought were mysteries, his knowledge of people before he met them, his assignments being the exact thing I would run in to, his bible verse, his talk of future pain from tragedy. He could have stopped this, he allowed one of the people that supported him the most perish! I pull up to Omar's house screaming his name, I could see the lights come on from the neighboring houses. I bang on his door until my knuckles where tender. No lights came on inside, no sounds were heard inside and no one answered. I went to Mr. Taylors spot and the church all coming up empty. It seemed the SG was concealing him from me!

"Omar!!" I yelled to the heavens in the middle of the street. In my mind his words had done something that years in the streets didn't, kill Roman.

Stone

The radio is on fire with yet another shooting! What was going on! There was no need to go to the victim because the victim was coming to me at the hospital. The elevator could not have been more slow, I ran down the stairs skipping two, three at a time. By the time I got to the other emergency room by badge had no power as I was denied entry. I tried to get a good look at the face in the mirror when I realized it was the very person I was attempting to see tonight!

So much blood had been spilled that martial law seemed to be the answer. With Tone still on the loose it was only a matter of time before he himself would end up dead! I walk back over to the room where Ali was, the doctors where still profusely working on him. Finally, the nurse came back with Ali's belongings in a plastic bag, a cell phone, wallet and a picture of his daughter.

The picture mesmerizes me, The beautiful little girl was a picture I had not looked at because I was too busy analyzing her corpse photos. I tap the phone on to find an entry code required. The phone companies would have to be the ones to unlock the device. Just as I was putting the evidence away Ali's phone rings. The caller ID has one name, Ross.

Cordell

I couldn't believe his stupid ass made such a scene. He better fuckin answer this phone. The back ground becomes available and my anger immediately shoots words at him.

"What part of low profile don't you understand!!! What happen to the silencer why are there witnesses saying shots were heard! You had the drop and you blew it! Look Stone is going to be all over this case we need distance apart, don't say nothing about me and I will make sure this goes away."

At that moment the TV show turns to breaking news and I see Ali's picture with the other victims of the shooting. The person who answered the phone was not who I thought it was.

"Cordell you are finished. Turn yourself in so you can make it easier on yourself." With that the phone hung up. My body fell to the ground when I had finally realized what I had done! Why the hell hadn't I had let him say hello first! My emotion had made me so stupid that I had buried my own grave.

The bottle of Jack Daniels warms my body as the cold reality hits. I smoke 6 cigarettes in a row trying to indulge in any buzz I can before the building falls on top of me. I think about why I went this route, the money I gained had been spent of shit that wouldn't give me any gain. The messed up part about it is the very people I served by to protect me against these animals was the same people that were going to lock me in a cage like one. The police will be here any minute and I know the dead end is near. I find it hard to distinguish if I would rather have man punish me verses God as I place the 9 mm to my head.

Time seems to travel so fast as 20 minutes had already pass before I saw the red and blue lights through my window. They think they are going to take me in huh. One thing I did learn in the streets is that you go out on your own terms. I finish the rest of the bottle and walk to the door. I twist the handle knowing my life is done but not before my final act.

"Fuck you!" I yelled kicking upon the door and squeezing the trigger as many times as I could before my body wasted away in the fire from friends I had worked side by side with.

Chapter 27

Tone

My stomach is talking to me but I can't talk back. My face is splattered across town and I can't just walk into a store. My companions have alienated themselves from me saying I'm too hot. I should have known the heat would get to hot for me. In every movie I see the king pin always has his day. The air is cool out here however, the smell of pine cones is over powering a pleasant difference from smelling car exhaust all day. My time of freedom is running out like the sand in an hour glass. I contemplate if taking me life is better than facing the music or being on the run the rest of my time. I shudder at the thought of what awaits me with my sin count at an all-time high.

I didn't want to shoot Rome, I never thought he would die by my hands, when I threaten him I had no intention behind it. You just can't quit my nigga! You can't just say I'm done with this and get your picked fence house and a family. If niggas like me had that option it would had been done. Rome knew what it was and he just kept coming at me, what was I supposed to do? Kill or be kill that's the code, I didn't make the shit up its just how the world works.

My justifications give me little relief to the guilt of executing Rome, Scoobie perished before his time because of my actions. I killed Bone because I didn't want to end up right in the position I'm in now. Maybe I should had let Bone just end it, at least cats would still be breathing. My thoughts trace back further to the point it all started because of my ambition. My ambition to control everything, my business was lucrative enough and yet I still go take Ali's territory. For years, our businesses never impeded each other's. He had his zone I had mine and yet I felt his area was mine because I deserve more money. My ambition is the mask that greed wears and I wonder if it was my bullet that hit the little girl. It was my call that started it all and the ripple effect claimed so many lives. My greed had people killed and had me sleep with my best friend's lady! For the first time, I see myself as a monster with no mirror required.

I hear twigs cracking and bushes rustling behind. What the hell who the fuck comes down here, nobody comes down hear I thought. I immediately duck down in a pile of bushes with a fallen down log. Me running for it would definitely cause to much noise and they would alert the police if it wasn't them to begin with. My hiding position allows me a view of who is approaching and my eyes are in disbelief.

Omar

I never tell my son about this location, hell I never told him anything in life. I don't understand why I would think to look here, I'm sure he bailed out of town. I still walk the invisible trail to an opening and think if my words went too far. The change I was preaching about is one that would put my son out of business and cause the community to turn on him. Before my words, Andre had a steady stream of revenue and fear from others that he probably thought was respect. I should had approached him first and try to reach out to him. My mind questions sista Aamira's judgment as I stand still amongst mother nature.

"What the fuck is you doing here"

The sound appeared out of nowhere. There in the bushes next the log rose my son.

"Looking for you." I responded.

"Nigga you aint the law and I'm not active any more so as far as your concern I'm not a threat to you. I suppose your going to call the police." He said pulling a gun out and aiming it at my head.

"Naw, me and the police have different words for you, but I'm sure you will answer them one day. I just had to meet you."

"Meet me? Nigga I don't want to meet you, shouldn't you be at a church somewhere preachin. Nigga you turned my best friend against me with the shit you was talking about but you see you don't….."

"Know what." I interrupted. "I don't know how these streets are, I don't know what is like to not have anything, or I don't know what it is like to be hungry." He stood there frozen, I can tell by his posture that he is trying to figure me out. The barrel still points to my head as I walk closer.

"You inherited more than just my genes but sadly my way of life I use to live."

"What! Nigga what the fuck you mean my genes!" he questions.

"You wouldn't know because I was locked up and your mother felt it best not to see me in a cage, which I can't fully say was a bad idea."

Tone

The absent was now standing right in front of me and my very demise I had in my targets. I always wondered what I would do if I ever knew my real father and I always imagine what he be like. It doesn't matter anymore! Time to make up is long gone and my shock turns to anger.

"Now! You come now! What I'm supposed to do bond with you nigga! You up here preaching to everyone else but you don't stop by and announce yourself to me, when the heat is on me that's when you want to introduce yourself? Man how the fuck did you even know to find me here!?"

He stood silent for a moment but my impatience didn't allow him the option to take his sweet time.

"Nigga answer me!" I said cocking the hammer back on my 9.

"I used to come here all the time Andre and take in the wilderness. I found a place where I could think and vent from my dramatic life. I was hungry Andre, a hunger pain that couldn't be cured with just a sandwich. I choose the same path just as you did and took what I thought was mine and cursed anybody who got in my way or had something to say. I felt their privilege voided their comments and if you came from the same back ground I did with an opposing argument I looked at them as weak. The bullets, drugs, and money brought me the life I wanted and I thought my sins would go uncollected but sooner or later you pay for the things you do. Your mother found out she was pregnant and I was ecstatic, I was going to give you everything and raise you just like them TV kids; but family and streets don't mix.

Family clouds your judgment on the streets and the streets steal your love ones which was a lesson I learned to late.

Uncontrolled emotion drove me down a dark path when I pulled a gun similar to the one your holding now and put it to his chest. We had just transported a large amount of drugs and cashed out and life couldn't have been any higher. Word got around that I had some possible loose ends in my operation and a finger got pointed at my right hand. I wasn't thinking Andre, he was guilty before words spilled out of his mouth. I pulled the trigger Andre! The worst part I felt numb, I didn't feel pain. It wasn't long before my actions came to light and the police came crashing through the door and throwing me in a cage. That was 26 years ago Andre and I know it's too late to be your father but you have the opportunity to repent. Guilt will eat you alive Andre, especially when you're in a cell with your thoughts. Jail is inevitable, to many things have been done Andre I'm not going to sugar coat it but you must change your mind set. You have blocked out all morality so that you can be full, and hunger confuses ambition with greed.

Andre your mentality of being societies victim has forfeited your option to becoming a survivor. And because of that mind set you believe scavenging of off others is surviving. Your hands have brought pain and death and you do all this just to feed yourself. I wasn't there to tell you those things as a child but as a man I can't answer for you only you can despite your troubled past. Running from your consequences is only delaying the inevitable and when you delay the penalty gets bigger. Put down your gun and let go of your pain because your pain is now being spread to others. Your dark world creates more children just like you, Romans child now has no father just like you did, Ali's daughter is dead just like what happened to your sister and the cycle of pain continues." He's at point blank range from my gun when he completes his last thought. I knew he was right. The person I had just met gave me more insight than every person that spoke a word to me.

I pick up my phone and call the first person I need to get the process started.

Stone

The coffee taste bitter today but I still sip it out of habit. My energy is at full mass but I crave the caffeine. The cases keep piling up on my desk and yet the one case I desire to solve is coming up short. I understand why many people acted like they didn't see anything because life was taken if someone breathed towards law enforcement. I used to curse the community I served believing they were cowards when they were merely trying to not be the next victim. I never knew danger until I joined the force. My community was tight nit while many children in the SG have to worry about wearing the wrong color.

Every lead goes cold on the pursuit of Andre. He had become more famous than ever with his picture splattered around the state. Family and friends didn't know his where abouts or were unwilling to corporate. The night of all those deaths was titled the Red Saturday and a night that is forever branded in my head. That week went down in Saints Grove history as the bloodiest week. The victims of that night where all victims to more than just the bullet that claimed them, but society itself. The little girl was a child taken by her father's mistakes, Roman because he tried to change his life to fast, Bone because he was ready to come clean, Isaiah for idolizing the wrong person, Michael aka Scoobie for being a loyal companion and Cordell for stumbling on his own greed. Societies played a part in all these deaths. That week changed my life and my perception on the black community.

Generations upon generations of oppression can never be wiped out just because a new generation is born. The ideology of self-preservation has tainted the black man's view on his own fellow man. Unity is a luxury that are privileged to other races but for blacks it's after their own self is preserved before one worries about the person next to them. Even in this sea of opportunity the black community finds itself drowning and boats constantly passes them by. Cordell although played a villain was a victim in his own right. The hatred and superior ideology was inherited by his ancestors and is sadly passed on to one generation to the other. He thought of the blacks as inferior being's incapable of changing and thus justified him taking advantage of their situation for his benefit.

Not to say that I have sympathy for people who break the law but I wouldn't be telling the truth if I didn't feel for their situation. My soft chair along with the prolong sitting wears on me and I have to stand up. Romans funeral is today and I debate if I should go. I went to each of the memorials including Cordells. I grab my coat from around my chair when my office phone rings.

"Detective Stone how may I help you"

"Meet me at lakeside cemetery in 3 hours" with that the phone went dead. His voice had a tone that only one person could carry.

Darrius

There were no more meetings the days that followed, no more of Omar's speeches. It seemed just as he magically appeared he had mysteriously vanished. Saints Grove started to decline form the neighborhood and was starting to turn back into the hood that consumed this community. It seemed that Omar's words had only hyped the people up but hadn't changed them. It had changed me back to who I was, I had fallen back into the cycle of work, and school to hopefully get better work. I didn't even dream anymore.

The funeral was set today and I had fell into a deep slump. I walked up to the church and saw the mass off people bigger than the crowd at Omar's speeches combined. I shook my head, only tragedy brought us together not triumph, God help us I thought.

I was the closet person to Roman. Although we were cousins we had the bond of brothers. Roman and I were like a shadow to a body so it felt weird walking around with just myself. I saw everyone here and couldn't remember the last time Roman even saw these people except in maybe passing by. I knew many people were here for show, I walked out the back of the church to get some air. I had to give the elegy so I had to calm my nerves, public speaking had never come natural to me. Through the waffle iron fence, I couldn't believe who I saw coming up.

2 Tone was walking with a group of people towards the church. My fist clenched so hard that I bruised my own hand. I got up ready to avenge my fallen brother. Before my hand could reach the fence gate a warm hand grabbed my forearm.

There he was in the flesh wearing his usual black attire perfect for today's festivities it seemed. Fire filled my eyes as I grabbed a hand full of his black cotton shirt and drove him hard into the brick building!

"What the hell are you doing here! You knew about this the whole time, you could had saved him! You could had saved him! You talk all that shit about saving this damn community and yet you don't save the one person who followed your teaching the hardest! I don't know what you are or where you came from but I do know your more than just an Omar, I finally had time to put all this shit together and know that somehow some way you could had stopped Roman! And where the hell have you been!"

I yelled every last word trying my best not to unload my fists in his face. The tears streamed down my face and I was ready to transfer all my hate towards Omar.

"I know it hurts Darrius I know.."

"Shut the hell up! You don't know shit cause you all talk! You don't know how I feel and if you did know how I feel there is no way in hell you would allow me to feel this way cause I wouldn't want anybody to feel this!"

"I know, war is hard Darrius. Roman was a strong man that was all in. I hate how our people are. She said that tragedy brings our people together more than anything. Now I didn't plan this but I can't let you fall back into hate. You're ready to give up on your people, possibly turn. You can't we have to be stronger than the cowards that are afraid of change! The people who shot Roman can't keep winning, we can't retract to fear!"

"What did you say?"

"I said we can't…"

"No….you said she, who is she?"

"Asalamalakim brother Darrius" A soft voice came from behind me. I turned around to see the Muslim lady dressed in all white.

"What I don't get it, you planned all this?"

"Murder? No, I believe life should be cherished to the last breath. I did know that these words would shake the mountain. My voice wouldn't had been heard by the masses but Omar's thunderous voice would command attention. I didn't know Roman would be the one to fall but I do know that he knew the streets and understood the risk. The price for this audience and the lessons Omar spoke could only be paid for with a life. That's a price Roman felt was worth it. You can't hate the streets Darrius, you must be merciful and teach these people. If you hate them they will hate you back but if you love them they will change."

My grip surrendered Omar's shirt, "So all these assignments and Omar's speeches, that was you?"

"My wording yes but it was all of our efforts that brought this town so far."

"What do you mean brought the town so far, look we still murdering, you call this progress." I yelled.

"I see an audience out there that mourns the loss of a fallen hero. I see the person that you were about to battle that struck you family member down in the audience. I to felt the same way when my granddaughter was taken from this world, but she was taken away from a sickness. A sickness that affects even healthy people if in the wrong place at the wrong time. The streets have a sickness that needs to be cured. Sadly, my granddaughter started this for me and Roman has started it for you but know that this illness has affected our people long before us. I see people more vulnerable than ever ready to see change and that is exactly what all these writing assignments have been preparing you for to spread the message." She preached

My heart ached for my loss but my body felt oddly relaxed, The weight on my shoulders had eased making me feel light on my feet. My restless gasping turned into fluid breathing and my eyes that had been blurred with tears where now sharp and focused. I looked at my watch and saw that it was time to take the stage. I headed towards the back entrance and turned around just before I entered.

"I never got your name."

She looked at me with the same smile she had always given me. "Aamira Abdullah."

Chapter 28

Darrius

I stood looking amongst the sea of eyes, ears that were ready to hear memories of Roman or a passage from the good book. I looked down at the podium. The microphone captured my breathing and the room grew silent with only the shifting in seats, clearing of throats and sniffling of noses. I could have sworn the audience heard my heart beat as it was pounding out of my chest. My internal body heat formed pools of sweat beneath my clothes. I look down at the coffin beside me and see his calm face, peaceful looking. His body would be buried in this coffin till the end of time and yet he seemed freer than anybody moving about. His frozen chest calmed mine down. I looked up and spoke.

"Roman spent his last moments fighting. He wasn't fighting for his life neither, he was fighting for you. He was fighting for the dormant potential that stays locked up! He was fighting the mentality of the stereotypical black man and woman. Most of you knew Roman as an infection in the community he was living in, you knew him as the example of what not to be. But if you had the pleasure to know him these past seven days he would had been a stranger to his old self. Roman learned more about himself in a week than he had his whole life. You see we assume the identities people give us. If you call a person smart his whole life, he will believe in that. If u call a person dumb his whole life, he will embrace that as well. You see Roman was called a nigga his whole life, not student, good man or child of god but a nigga.

Before this last week the music that played in his car drilled nigga in his brain, his friends all called him this, I at a point in time referred to him as that. Like so many of our lost brothers they live according to their titles. Because a real nigga does what he wants despite the consequences, a real nigga don't let a bitch get away with what they want, a real nigga get money by any means and if a real nigga gotta do time than so be it. Up until last week Roman finally heard his other titles. He heard brother, king, and strong black man. Up until last week he found out that his hood, block and ghetto was also called a community, and family. He heard his bitches and hoes called ladies, professionals and sisters. Finally, he found out that working in crime or working for another never owning anything no matter how much you make isn't freedom, its parole where u must keep checking in to protect your privileges.

Roman found out our ancestors didn't finish the job. We own our physical bodies but still fail to own our lives. The black community these days have forgotten that we are one people. All throughout our history in America we have been forced to divide and fight amongst ourselves. The practice of being separated created an environment to where the black people choose to be divided. We were not forced like the olden times. We were not permitted to read back in slavery but now we choose not to read and skip school. We were only permitted to use our bodies as labor to make money for others instead of our mind during slavery and now we choose to only use our physical attributes to make it instead of our intellect. Woman expose their bodies to get attention instead of their character. Many people only look at a lady's picture instead of the words they post. A woman speaking her mind receives far less likes than a woman dancing half naked. Young brothers broadcast middle fingers and nonproductive activities instead of business projects. Roman found all this out this last week.

Roman found out that he was doing more destruction to his people than the police were. He found out that our ignorance was doing us more harm than any other white man. He found out that us not even trying to our own work and homes was us picking up the chains and placing it on our own wrists. Roman died trying to reverse what we created. His last words were words of wisdom to his killer. In the black community killer is usually a synonym for brother but his last words were I told you I had changed.

The majority of you all didn't know Roman. Just like the minority of you all don't truly know the state of our black community. We don't own our businesses, hospitals, schools, merchandise, homes, banks, music, or lives. We don't even own our own history as it is lost in history. So, because most our people will never know where we originated from the next best thing is to assume that we all come from the same ancestors. We all are brothers and sisters and thus must stop fighting amongst each other. We must build together, invest in each other and preserve our lives together instead of taking lives from each other!

I hope one day you will know the black community and thus yourselves. Only when you know that will you truly know Roman." I stepped back from the microphone and was immediately confronted with the crowds approval.

The audience roared echoing it seemed throughout the world. I could feel the wolves awaking howling at the moon of opportunity. I looked over at Omar to see him smiling. I looked back at the audience and could see that Romans death gave life to the community. I walked down from the stage and looked at Roman one last time before the pastor came behind me to close it. My hands were confiscated by other hands and my body was being embraced left and right. "Thank you God," "yes Lord" and "Amen brother" filled the room.

The energy lasted all the way up until the casket began being lowered into the ground. Tears were coming down all cheeks. The tips of my fingers were cold and wet with sweat. My heart rattled my rib cage and my air felt thin. My throat became a desert causing it to itch. My legs became fatigue and I dropped down to my knees. My eyes flooded!

"Roman! Stop!!! Stop!!! Pull him up! Pull him up!" I cried.

My wife grabbed me "Baby he isn't here, He flew to heaven!"

"No no nooo!!!! Pull him up!"

My pleading cries turned into a steady sob until it was interrupted by the dirt hitting the casket. They were burying my family, my best friend. I looked around and everybody had left except my wife and Aamira.

"Im sorry sir we waited as long as we could we have to fill it in." Said one of the diggers.

"It's okay I will take it from here, sweetie if you could please go rest your feet in the car I will settle Darrius and bring him to you momentarily" Aamira directed.

Chelsea kisses my forehead and headed to the car.

"Darrius remember what you talked about today. Many times, we live to avoid an inevitable death and follow a path until we can't no more instead building a legacy that last for many life times and explore our own paths. You honor Roman by preventing others from following in the same path of his past and you do that by establishing sense of ownership and responsibility in your community. Close your eyes Darrius and here is the answer you have been waiting on. One of my plans has always been to completely wake up the black people."

My eye lids snapped open and I turned around so hard it gave me whip lash. She was gone, I turned all the way around, no sign of her. I knew who it was, God finally answered me for what he had instore for the black people. Another figure started walking towards me, As the figure grew closer I knew who it was.

There I was standing face to face with the man who took one of the closes people to me. 2 Tones eyes seemed blood shot but not from weed, this was from sleepless tearful nights.

"Man I aint come her for forgiveness because I know we way past that. It's just this shit is all I know. Roman was the best of me, and when it came to havin my back none came close. Shit just happen so fast, I didn't mean to shoot him it's just the argument got to real, I was off that liquor and did something I can't take back. Look before I dip I just needed to give you this."

It was an old picture of the three of us when we were younger, I couldn't help but smile at us back then.

"So what you just dip out of town, show me a pic and I'm just supposed to remember the good times? I mean is this what you think Roman would be cool with? You killed him Andre and that's not something a pic can heal, not even close."

Andre smiled, "I didn't say I was the one driving. I gave them my location and all the locations of my product, connections and stash houses. I'm out the game like Roman tired to get me to do.

Right after Andre announced that two squad cars pull up alongside of the road. With guns drawn they rushed to our location and directed Andre with a series of commands until he was subdued right in front of the grave site of Roman. "It looks like its my time, keep fighting Darrius you can hate me but keep fighting, give my own kids a better shot at living life." he announced.

I saw Roman, Aamira and Omar for the last time that day.

I drive back from the grave yard site reminiscing on the memories with my fallen brother all while talking with my father on the phone. I tell him that I'm going to write about this and show our people what's really going on. We go back and forth about a title before I finally find an excuse to get off the phone. I pull up to my apartment walk through the door to a place empty and I pull the dining room chair out. I pull out my note book with all my writing assignments, open my laptop and can think of nothing else to key in. I take a deep breath and type…..WAKE UP!!

Author

Native to Seattle Washington, Deon Abdullah served in the United States Air Force from 2009-2015 earning two associate degrees in criminal justice. He is married to Nahstassia Abdullah and together they have three children, Nia, Cameron and Amyr Abdullah.

His debut book explores different perspectives in the African American community both inside and outside. Living in different environments Deon was able to acquire an in-depth understanding on the different philosophies, ideologies and cultures of different sub groups within the African American community. These different views tied in with the lack of business and real state ownership creates obstacles in the progression of Blacks.

This inspired Deon to write his first book and enter the fight for social equality.

www.ingramcontent.com/pod-product-compliance
Lightning Source LLC
Chambersburg PA
CBHW020734180526
45163CB00001B/239